Everyday Classroom Strategies and Practices for Supporting Children With Autism Spectrum Disorders

Jamie D. Bleiweiss, PhD, Lauren Hough, MsEd, and Shirley Cohen, PhD

©2013 AAPC Publishing
P.O. Box 23173
Shawnee Mission, Kansas 66283-0173
www.aapcpublishing.net

Publisher's Cataloging-in-Publication

Bleiweiss, Jamie D.
      Everyday classroom strategies and practices for supporting children with autism spectrum disorders / Jamie D. Bleiweiss, Lauren Hough, and Shirley Cohen. -- Shawnee Mission, Kan. : AAPC Publishing, c2013.

            p. ; cm.

            ISBN: 978-1-937473-81-5
            LCCN: 2013940030
            A manual on classroom practices to supplement "The ASD nest model" (AAPC Publishing, c2013).
            Includes bibliographical references.
            Summary: Evidence-based classroom practices for supporting students with autism spectrum disorders in the general education classroom. Companion volume to "The ASD nest model: a framework for inclusive education for higher functioning children with autism spectrum disorders."--Publisher.

      1. Autistic children--Education--Handbooks, manuals, etc. 2. Autism spectrum disorders--Patients--Education--Handbooks, manuals, etc. 3. Teachers of children with disabilities--Handbooks, manuals, etc. I. Hough, Lauren. II. Cohen, Shirley, 1937- III. Title. IV. Title: ASD nest model.

LC4717.5 .B54 2013
371.94--dc23   1306

This book is designed in Frutiger.

Cover design by Rex Huang.

Printed in the United States of America.

Dedication

To the staff of ASD Nest programs at schools
throughout the five boroughs of New York City
who use the strategies and supports in this manual every day,
and especially to Dorothy Siegel, whose intensive drive
turned the idea of an inclusion program for children with autism
spectrum disorders into the reality of the ASD Nest program.
And finally, to the children and families who provided us
with evidence of the goodness-of-fit
of the strategies and supports we used every day.

Acknowledgments

We wish to thank the central staff of consultants to the ASD Nest program for their myriad contributions to the practices presented in this manual, in particular Angela Mouzakitis, Susan Brennan, Kristie Koenig, Gizem Tanol, and Aaron Lanou. We are also grateful to Brenda Smith Myles and Kirsten McBride at AAPC Publishing for their support throughout the process of producing this manual.

The ASD Nest program reflects a long collaborative process involving two university colleges – New York University's Steinhardt School of Culture, Education and Human Development, and Hunter College of the City University of New York – and the New York City Department of Education. We wish to thank the administrators of all three institutions who supported and contributed to this relationship so that the ASD Nest program could be established and continue its work with children on the autism spectrum.

Table of Contents

Preface

Shirley Cohen

Everyday Classroom Strategies and Practices for Supporting Children With Autism Spectrum Disorders was conceptualized in the spring of 2012 after the manuscript of the book The ASD Nest Model: A Framework for Inclusive Education for Higher-Functioning Children With Autism Spectrum Disorders was completed and submitted to AAPC Publishing. That book provides the structure or "bones" of the ASD Nest program along with the story of how it was created, a sampling of the content of the program, and a general picture of how it was doing. A description of the students served by the ASD Nest, the professional development program that undergirds the ASD Nest, the challenges in sustaining an inclusion program for children with ASD within a large urban school system, and the voices of parents of children served by this program are also included in that book. The book gives district and school administrators, supervisors, advocates, and parents a template for what an effective inclusion program serving higher-functioning children with autism spectrum disorders (ASD) might look like, how it could be established, and how it might operate.

While that book delineates an overall approach and samples of strategies for the classroom, we realize that many teachers would benefit from more than that – from a stronger focus on everyday classroom practices designed to meet the needs of children with ASD. That realization led to the production of this manual on classroom practices. The manual can be used as a companion to the book for everyone involved in the education and treatment of children with ASD, and for classroom teachers and their support teams, it can also stand alone. Chapter 1 is a brief overview for readers who are not familiar with the ASD Nest program that was presented in The ASD Nest Model.

Chapter 1

Introduction

Shirley Cohen

One can barely read the news these days without encountering some mention of autism, usually communicating alarm about its increased prevalence or the myriad possible factors, genetic and environmental, that may cause or trigger it. Parents-to-be and parents of infants are frightened. Well-known figures from the entertainment field are lending themselves to fundraising efforts for research into this condition. Conferences on autism abound. Arguments about diagnosis and labeling pervade the medical and educational fields. Should the term "autism spectrum disorder" have replaced the terms "autistic disorder, Asperger's disorder, and pervasive developmental disorder-not otherwise specified (PDD-NOS) in the latest version of the widely used diagnostic manual of the American Psychiatric Association (DSM-5)? What genes cause autism? And finally, what treatments and/or supports that are available now will help which children the most?

It is this last question that this manual and the book associated with it, *The ASD Nest Model* (Cohen & Hough, 2013), address. The co-founders (Dorothy Siegel and Shirley Cohen), consultants, and long-term staff of the ASD Nest program have developed and have been implementing an intervention model for higher-functioning children with autism spectrum disorders (ASD) that has enabled almost all of the children in this program to be successfully educated in classes with their more typically developing peers in neighborhood public schools. While providing support for the special needs of these children, we are strengthening their ability to understand and meet social and academic expectations.

Who are these "higher functioning" children with ASD?

They are children who have challenges in social communication and interactions along with restricted and repetitive patterns of behavior, interests, and activities. Many are highly routine-dependent and resistant to change. Some have unusual reactions to sensory stimuli, with hypersensitivity to one or more types of sensory input. Some have poor self-regulation and frequent meltdowns. Others need extra time to process verbal communications and respond to them. Many are highly anxious. Some flap their hands or jump up and down when they are anxious or excited. And many are passionately interested in selected subjects and are intellectually curious as well as creative. Virtually all have IQs within the range considered average or higher, and all have received a diagnosis of autism, either prior to being considered for admission to the ASD Nest program or during the admission process. Most children are admitted at kindergarten age, with a few being admitted in higher grades when there are openings in the program.

The strategies and classroom practices described in this manual were designed for the ASD Nest program. The ASD Nest model is an inclusion program serving children who have ASD, particularly higher-functioning children with that condition. As of the 2012-2013 school year, the ASD Nest program was being implemented in 19 public elementary schools in New York City. While the program serves children on the autism spectrum who are often referred to as high-functioning or "higher-functioning," many of the practices in this book will be useful in working with children with ASD who are not usually thought of as higher functioning, as well as other populations of children with special needs, including children identified as having attention deficit hyperactivity disorder (ADHD) and children with learning or behavior disorders.

The principles behind these practices take into consideration each child's needs, strengths, and interests, all basic to sound and effective instruction in both general and special education.

The ASD Nest model includes the structural elements listed below. (For more extensive information about this model, see *The ASD Nest Model* [Cohen & Hough, 2013]). Many, if not most, of the discrete strategies recommended in this manual can also be utilized in programs that do not include all the structural elements of the ASD Nest model, provided that an overall framework of positive behavior support exists.

- **Reduced class size:** 12 students at the kindergarten level, 4 of them children with ASD; 16 students in grades 1-3, 4 of them with ASD; up to 20 students in grades 4-5, up to 5 of them with ASD

- **Co-teaching:** two classroom teachers, one certified in special education and one in general early childhood or childhood education, or teachers certified in both special education and general early childhood or childhood education; plus a cluster teacher, who divides her time between ASD Nest classes to support children during special subjects and instructional lunch

- **A transdisciplinary team approach** with weekly team meetings that include teachers, related service providers (speech-language pathologist, occupational therapist, social worker), and a school administrator (principal or assistant principal)

- **A central team of ASD consultants** – positive behavior support specialists, speech-language pathologists, and special educators with a focus on ASD, who work with participating schools during their first two years in the program and on an "as-needed" basis after that. (In some schools that have been in the program for more than two years, the consultant is replaced by a "coach/cluster teacher;" that is, an experienced ASD Nest teacher who has received additional training and is provided with several periods for coaching each week.)

- **Targeted goal areas:** social understanding and social communication, self-regulation and coping skills, adaptive behavior, selected academic skills needed by individual students in order to meet grade expectations

- **Use of intervention strategies delineated in the Classroom Guideposts for the ASD Nest program and the Three-Tier Model of Supports for the ASD Nest program**, which are presented later in this manual. (In addition, there is a social development intervention focus, SDI, led by each program's speech-language pathologist, consisting of sessions that take place outside the classroom daily at the kindergarten level and three times a week at higher grade levels.)

- **Preservice training** consisting of two graduate courses focused on ASD taken at Hunter College in the summer prior to beginning work in the ASD Nest program

- **Inservice training** during the school year through workshops and conferences led by the consultants to the ASD Nest Support Project at New York University

- **Home-school connection:** home and school visits for new students before the start of the school year; two-way communication notebooks; school-based parent meetings; workshops and conferences

Permeating all elements of the ASD Nest program is an overall framework of positive behavior support and a welcoming, supportive atmosphere.

The ASD Nest Program Classroom Guideposts

The Classroom Guideposts document is a compendium of strategies and practices that are basic to the ASD Nest model and are used frequently in all classes in the program. Many of the strategies have a strong evidence base in relation to students with ASD while others are considered highly promising, and still others are accepted as best practice in special education. These practices focus on the needs and challenges common to children with ASD (Smith, Myles, Aspy, Grossman, & Henry, 2010; Stansberry-Brusnahan & Collet-Klingenberg, 2010). However, the way Guidepost practices are implemented varies depending on age/grade differences between classrooms. Use of these strategies and practices is guided by team planning for both individual students and whole classes.

The Classroom Guideposts are organized into five categories that have guided our thinking about intervention: prevention strategies, instructional strategies and supports, social supports, teaching replacement behavior, and positive reinforcement systems. However, these categories are not mutually exclusive, as some practices can be and are used for multiple purposes.

The Classroom Guideposts are introduced to new staff of the ASD Nest program during their summer training program prior to beginning work in the program, and they are also used as a resource in planning for classes and for individual students throughout the school year. The Guideposts are expanded periodically as new strategies and practices are identified that are consistent with the overall approach of the model and have been found to be beneficial to students in the program. The latest version of the Classroom Guideposts is presented in Chapter 2.

Three-Tier Model of Supports for the ASD Nest Program

The Three-Tier Intervention Model, the ASD Nest version of a response-to-intervention (RTI) system (Fuchs, Fuchs, & Compton, 2012; Van DerHeyden & Burns, 2010), provides guidelines for which strategies and practices from the Classroom Guideposts to use with which students and when. The three tiers are defined by frequency and intensity of service delivery and by the level of direct adult involvement. Each tier is organized into four domains: behavioral, social, academic, and sensory functioning/self-regulation supports.

The ASD Nest Three-Tier Model differs from the broader use of RTI in that all tiers in the ASD Nest system are designed for use with special education students, particularly students with ASD. Thus, Tier I is designed to be used with all students in inclusion classes – both children on the autism spectrum and their more typically developing peers. Tier II is used for students with ASD (or other special needs) for whom the practices at Tier I are insufficient to help them meet individualized education program (IEP) goals or program expectations. This tier consists of individualized strategies and supports that are implemented in small groups, sometimes with initial teaching in a one-to-one format. Finally, Tier III is designed for students who have major difficulty in meeting expectations even after Tier II strategies have been used for some time.

The intensive, highly individualized supports in Tier III are only used after careful assessment by the school team and an ASD Nest program consultant, as well as a meeting with a child's parent. Practices in Tier III are substantially more intensive than those of Tiers I and II, and they require much one-to-one teaching, support, and monitoring. As a result, they may reduce the amount of teacher support that can be given to other students, and are therefore generally used only when a student is at risk of being considered for movement to a more restrictive setting. Figure 1.1 presents the conceptual model of the ASD Nest Three-Tier system. The full model is presented in Chapter 3.

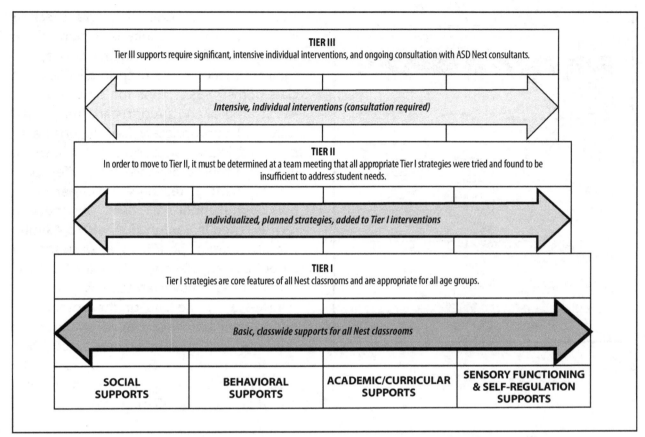

Figure 1.1. **Three-tier model of supports for the ASD Nest program.**

Just as the other major component of the program, the ASD Nest program Classroom Guide-posts, the Three-Tier ASD Nest Model is introduced to new staff of the ASD Nest program during their summer training, and is used in conjunction with the Classroom Guideposts in team planning both for classes and for individual students throughout the school year. Implementation of the Three-Tier Model is guided by the use of checklists. Four checklists have been designed to be used in this process.

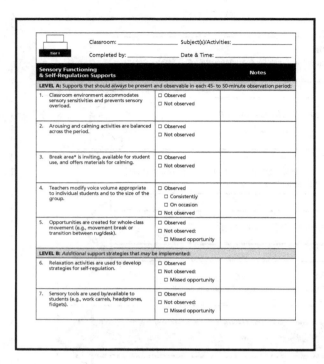

- **Tier I Classroom Checklist.** This checklist is used to monitor implementation of the strategies and supports in the Guideposts that are meant to be used in all ASD Nest classrooms. It is a tool for ensuring that the strategies and supports are being used fully and appropriately (i.e., to ensure fidelity of implementation). It can also be used as a tool to advance the professional development of teachers and other members of the school ASD team. This checklist is often used in conjunction with a 45-minute observation period by a consultant or school-based ASD coach. Completion of the checklist itself may then take as little as 10 minutes after the end of the observation period and before a discussion between the observer and the teachers takes place. The form may also be used by classroom teachers for self-study, which may involve anywhere from 30-45 minutes.

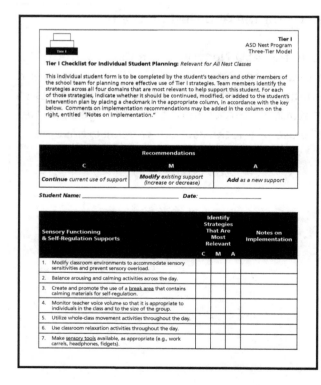

- **Tier I Checklist for Individual Student Planning.** This checklist is used by the team to identify strategies and supports within Tier I to plan more effective intervention for a child who is not moving toward meeting his IEP goals and class/grade expectations, or who is exhibiting behavior that interferes with learning. Teachers complete a draft of this checklist a short time before a case conference on the child is scheduled to take place. This process often takes about 20 minutes. That draft is then used as a starting point for a discussion by the team, which may take about 20 minutes.

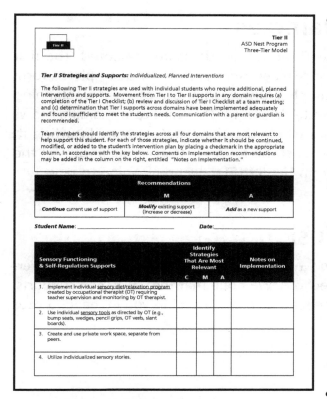

- **Tier II Checklist for Individual Student Planning.** This checklist consists of strategies and supports that are used in planning for a child for whom the strategies in Tier I have not been sufficient in helping to move the child toward meeting IEP goals and class/grade expectations or reducing interfering behavior, even after the implementation of the Tier I individual plan. Teachers use this checklist to review the effectiveness of the Tier I strategies and supports they have been using and to identify any additional supports they think may be useful by checking them on the Tier II planning form. This process may take about 20 minutes. That draft of the Tier II planning document then becomes a starting point for the team's case conference on the child, which may take an additional 20 minutes or so.

- **Tier III Checklist for Individual Student Planning.** This checklist is used in planning for a child for whom the strategies in Tiers I and II have not been sufficient in helping to move that child toward meeting IEP goals and class/grade expectations or reducing interfering behavior; and who is at risk of being moved to a more restrictive setting. This checklist is part of a comprehensive evaluation of an individual child, which invariably includes extensive data collection and additional data collection forms. The child's parent and an ASD program consultant must be involved when movement to Tier III strategies and supports is being considered. A functional behavior assessment is often conducted as part of the process of creating the Tier III intervention plan. While completion of the Tier III form, which takes place at the end of the evaluation process, does not take very long, the entire evaluation process may take anywhere from several days to about three weeks.

Complete versions and detailed descriptions of the above forms are found in Chapter 3.
In addition, owners of this book may download these and other forms and checklists from www.aapcpublishing.net/9105.

Case Examples

Chapter 4 presents case examples of how the Three-Tier Model is implemented. The first illustration focuses on use of the Tier I Classroom Guideposts and includes a completed form for a second-grade class. The second case example illustrates the use of Tier I in planning for an individual child in a different second-grade classroom. The third case example shows how Tier II can be used to support a student for whom the Tier I strategies are insufficient, leaving him struggling to meet school expectations. The fourth case example illustrates the process of considering a child for movement from Tier II to Tier III and planning to serve him or her at that most intense level.

Conclusion

This chapter highlighted the background from which this manual grew along with an overview of its major components and their intersections. We hope that the strategies, supports, and practices presented in the remainder of the manual prove useful to you in meeting your goals for helping children with ASD.

Chapter 2

Classroom Guideposts

This chapter focuses on the ASD Nest Program Classroom Guideposts, a major component of the program. Because the ASD Nest is an inclusion program that adheres to the basic curriculum of the school and grade, the Classroom Guideposts serve as the framework for the "other curriculum" essential for children with autism spectrum disorders (ASD).

This additional curriculum, sometimes referred to as a " hidden curriculum" (Myles, Trautman, & Schelvan, 2013), is a set of "rules" or general understandings that are not directly taught in school because everyone is assumed to know them – to have somehow come to understand them through general exposure to social situations and interactions with others. Examples include communicating differently to teachers than to peers; knowing how to greet someone you hardly know compared to someone you know well; engaging in turn-taking during conversations; and "reading" emotions from facial expressions.

The Classroom Guideposts also focus on strengthening children's skills – in self-regulation and coping with stress; in expanding interactions with peers and forming friendships; in tackling academic tasks that are particularly challenging to them; in finding ways to resolve problems that are not "off-putting" to others to replace those that are; and in coming to know and like themselves.

The strategies and supports in the Classroom Guideposts address areas of difficulty common in children with ASD, specifically sensory functioning, social communication and relatedness, self-regulation, management of anxiety, and selected cognitive processes. The ASD Nest Classroom Guideposts are presented in Figures 2.1-2.47. The later section of this chapter focuses on how to use the Guideposts.

Overview of ASD Nest Program

The ASD Nest elementary school program is an inclusion program for students with ASD from kindergarten through fifth grade housed in multiple public elementary schools in New York City. The ASD Nest Program Classroom Guideposts serve as the basic manual on strategies for the classroom, while the procedures for applying these strategies with individual children and classes is more fully explained in the Three-Tier Model, which is presented in Chapter 3.

The Guideposts are divided into five major sections, consisting of the following evidence-based practices:

1. Prevention strategies (sometimes known as antecedent-based interventions)

2. Instructional strategies and supports

3. Social supports

4. Teaching replacement behavior

5. Positive reinforcement systems

The ASD Nest program uses a positive behavior support (PBS) approach and incorporates strategies that address areas of difficulty common in children with ASD, specifically, sensory functioning, social relatedness, self-regulation, managing anxiety, and selective cognitive problems. The strategies are a combination of evidence-based and highly promising practices, reflect a coherent intervention framework, and are implemented in a systematic way bolstered by initial professional development training and periodic additional training experiences. Table 2.1 displays a list of the evidence-based practices that are utilized in the ASD Nest Program. The evidence-based practices are derived from three major reports trying to identify evidence-based practice for children and youth with ASD: National Professional Development Center on ASD (NPDC on ASD, 2009), National Autism Center (NAC; 2009), and Centers for Medicare and Medicaid Services (CMS, 2010).

The premise of the Guideposts is that school-based interventions can help many children with ASD succeed.

Table 2.1
Evidence-Based Practices Used in the ASD Nest Program

Strategy	Evidence Supporting the Practice
Visual Supports (schedules, task boards)	Bernard-Opitz & Haubler, 2011; Dettmer, Simpson, Myles, & Ganz, 2000; Lequia, Machalicek, & Rispoli, 2012; Mesibov, Browder, & Kirkland, 2002; Quill, 1997
Video Modeling	Bellini, & Akullian, 2007; Buggey, 2009; Shukla-Mehta, Miller, & Callahan, 2010
Choice-Making Opportunities	Bambara, Koger, Katzer, & Davenport, 1995; Shogren, Faggella-Luby, Jik Bae, & Wehmeyer, 2004
Peer-Mediated Interventions	Harper, Symon, & Frea, 2008; Owen-DeSchryver, Carr, Cale, & Blakeley-Smith, 2008; Zhang & Wheeler, 2011
Social Narratives	Delano & Snell, 2006; Kokina & Kern, 2010; Scattone, Tingstrom, & Wilczynski, 2006
Relaxation Techniques	Mullins & Christian, 2001; Reaven, Blakeley-Smith, Leuthe, Moody, & Hepburn, 2012; Steen & Zuriff, 1977
Functional Communication Training	Carr & Durand, 1985; Durand & Merges, 2001; Mancil, 2006; Reichle, Drager, & Davis, 2002
Positive Reinforcement Strategies	Horner et al., 2005; Kamps et al., 2011; Marcus & Vollmer, 1996; Matson & Taras, 1989; Piazza, Moes, & Fisher, 1996
Antecedent-Based Intervention	Dadds, Schwartz, Adams, & Rose, 1988; Schilling & Schwartz, 20024
Naturalistic Teaching	Koegel, Camarate, Koegel, Bea-Tall, & Smith, 1998; Koegel, Dyer, & Bell, 1987; Pierce & Schreibman, 1997
Self-Management	Koegel & Koegel, 1990; Koegel, Koegel, Hurley, & Frea, 1992; Pierce & Schreibman, 1994; Stahmer & Schreibman, 1992; Kern, Marder, Boyaijan, Elliot, & McElhattan, 1997
Functional Behavior Assessment	Buckley & Newchok, 2005; LaBelle & Charlop-Christy, 2002; Lucyshyn et al., 2007

Prevention Strategies

Prevention strategies are designed to keep interfering behavior from occurring or to minimize such behavior and its disruptive effects upon the child with ASD as well as the other students in the class. Such prevention strategies are extremely important in enabling children with poor self-regulation to achieve the modicum of calm alertness that is needed for learning while relevant skills are being developed.

Most of the prevention strategies included in the Guideposts are valuable for all students and reflect evidence-based teaching practices that have been tailored to more fully address the specific needs of children with ASD.

Basic Classroom Design

When setting up the classroom at the beginning of the school year, aim for a calm, soothing environment. Many children with ASD are hypersensitive to stimuli and can become overwhelmed by a room that is filled with materials. Others are easily distracted from assigned activities or tasks in such a classroom or have difficulty finding the materials they need at a particular time. This is especially true in kindergarten and at the beginning of the school year at any grade level. As much as possible, avoid the clutter that may be created by unnecessary furniture and materials or poorly organized materials. Figures 2.1 and 2.2 show examples of lower- and upper-elementary school classrooms in the ASD Nest Program. (For a comprehensive resource on setting up classroom spaces that support children with ASD, see Kabott & Reeve, 2010.)

Figure 2.1. Lower-grade elementary school classroom.

Figure 2.2. **Upper-grade elementary school classroom.**

Cover display areas. If you are going to cover your bulletin boards or other display areas such as doors or walls, use neutral tones or light/warm colors (e.g., light blue or green, cream); avoid bright colors, like orange or red, which may be too distracting and over-stimulating for some students with ASD. Figure 2.3 shows an example of covered display areas.

Figure 2.3. **Covered shelving.**

Set up special bulletin boards. Reserve a particular bulletin board or area of the room to display children's photographs as well as samples of work products relevant to current learning objectives. This will help communicate to the students that the room is their school home.

Display necessary instructional materials. Display only materials that are being used in a lesson or that are needed for ongoing reference. When materials are no longer being used for either of these purposes, place them out of sight or turn them around so that only a blank surface is visible. Use drop cloths to cover shelves holding items that may be distracting when those items are not to be used.

Consider point of view. Always be mindful of the child's visual point of view. Items to be used by children for reference should be easily viewable by them. Consider the height, size, and distance of the display from where children using these items are seated. For example, "word walls" to be referenced during writing should not be 9 or 10 feet from a child unless students are free to move up close to the wall to read it; nor should editing checklists or number boards be posted close to the ceiling of the room.

Demarcate workspaces. Clearly demarcate spaces for individual and group work, including learning centers, throughout the classroom.

Set up a break area. Each classroom should have a break area (sometimes referred to as a "calming corner" or "recharge center"), a set-off quiet area with a beanbag chair and tools for self-calming, such as headphones for listening and fidgets. See Figure 2.4 for an example of a break area.

Figure 2.4. Break area.

Additional Environmental Modifications to Address Sensory Sensitivities

Modify room lighting. Standard classroom lighting can be modified to better suit students' sensory needs. As appropriate, use non-fluorescent lights, use a limited number of ceiling lights, dim lights during selected activities, keep shades drawn on particularly sunny days, or position light-sensitive children away from areas in the classroom where the sun is brightest.

Minimize visual stimuli. Use dividers or study carrels to separate students from distractions in the room during tasks that students find particularly challenging. Student "offices," like that shown in Figure 2.5, can help minimize visual distractions.

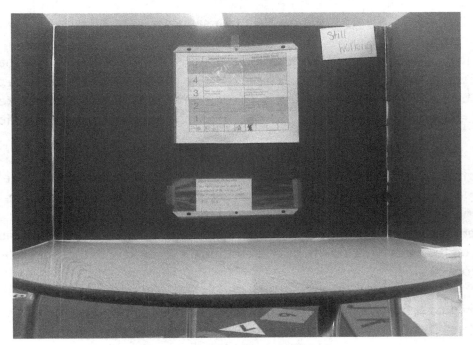

Figure 2.5. Student "office."

Address auditory sensitivities. Headphones can block out loud or disruptive noises to minimize auditory distractions during tasks that require concentrated attention. The Incredible 5-Point Scale (Buron & Curtis, 2012) can help students develop an awareness of their voice levels, for example (see page 24). Other supports include providing alternative tasks during crowded or noisy activities and using tennis balls or felt padding on the bottom of chair legs/movable furniture/equipment to minimize the loud scraping noises on the floor. See Figure 2.6 for an example.

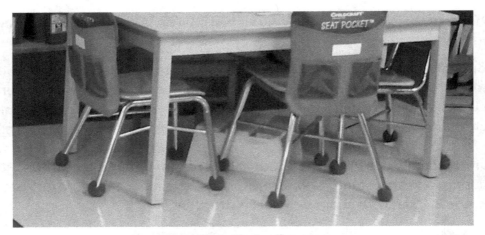

Figure 2.6. Chair silencers.

Use priming to give students advance notice about fire drills or loud bells (e.g., "We may have a fire drill today. If we do, what will we do? Let's practice so we will be ready."). In the case of a child still being upset by the fire bells after the class has been primed for fire drills, consider keeping headphones marked with his name or initials in a place where he can easily retrieve them for use during fire drills.

Address heightened needs for movement. Classrooms should provide enough space for students to move around and engage in vigorous physical activities such as dancing, jumping, and jogging in place during short movement breaks throughout the day. Try to plan the daily schedule so that activities alternate between sitting on the carpet and sitting at tables so that students are not expected to sit on the carpet in a modified yoga position (i.e., seated with their legs crossed in front) for long periods of time.

Address individual sensory/motor needs. Use adaptive materials and equipment such as adaptive seating (e.g., Disc-o-Sit; wedges; therapy ball chairs, available through many therapy resource websites such as www.Therapro.com) or weighted lap or shoulder cushions to address individual needs. Be sure to consult occupational therapists prior to implementing any adaptive equipment; in addition, inform parents about the use of and rationale for such equipment prior to its use with individual children. Sample sensory tools are shown in Figure 2.7.

Figure 2.7. Examples of sensory tools.

Basic Classroom Strategies and Tools

The following strategies should be part of the tool chest of every teacher working with children with ASD.

Visual supports. The use of visual aids such as pictures, words, and drawings may enable children with ASD, who tend to be better at visual than auditory processing, to function and succeed in the classroom. Visual supports provide students with increased predictability and help structure their environment, organize their day, and clarify expectations (Bernard-Opitz & Häußler, 2011; Dettmer, Simpson, Myles, & Ganz, 2000; Hodgdon, 1995).

Schedules and task boards

The use of visual schedules that depict upcoming events or the sequence of tasks in an activity has been found to be highly effective for students with ASD (Mesibov, Browder, & Kirkland, 2002; Quill, 1997).

Daily class schedule. A daily classroom schedule is a useful tool for assisting the many children with ASD who find their everyday world confusing, and thus crave predictability. Schedules should be clearly displayed for easy viewing and reference by students throughout the day and should outline the flow of the day's activities, with individual activity cards with written text and pictures as appropriate representing the activities. The activity cards should be detachable, so that as each activity is completed, the corresponding card can be removed, flipped over, or moved to a separate column that indicates that the activity is over. The daily schedule should be reviewed each morning and referred to after each activity to clarify what will come next and assist children with the transition to a different activity.

In the early part of the kindergarten year, the daily schedule of activities can overwhelm children by presenting more visual information than they can absorb at any one time. Therefore, it may be helpful to break up the schedule into "morning activities" and "afternoon activities," showing only the morning activities until lunchtime, at which point the afternoon activities are placed on the schedule. Figures 2.8 and 2.9 display examples of schedules for a lower-grade elementary and an upper-grade elementary classroom, respectively.

Morning Schedule!		
8:30		Unpack
8:45		Circle Time
9:15		Music
10:05		Snack
11:00	$123^{+\times}_{-\div}$	Math
11:40		Read-Aloud
12:00		Lunch

Figure 2.8. Sample classroom schedule for a lower-grade elementary school.

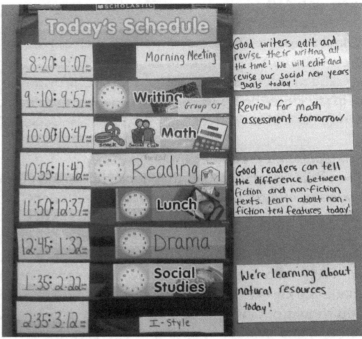

Figure 2.9. Sample classroom schedule for an upper-grade elementary school.

To avoid reinforcing the inflexibility that is present in most children with ASD, after the first few weeks of the year, vary the schedule to include a different experience once a week. Prepare children in advance by providing a picture of a question mark or of a mystery box on the daily schedule to indicate a surprise activity. See Figure 2.10.

Individualized mini-schedules. Individualized mini-schedules can be used with students who benefit from a more personalized schedule with a shorter sequence of activities than provided by the daily class schedule. Mini-schedules should consist of a written text and/or pictures representing three to four upcoming activities. See Figure 2.11.

The mini-schedule should be easily transportable and may be displayed on a small clipboard that the students carry with them throughout the day (e.g., on a small clipboard or velcroed™ into a notebook) to provide an additional form of support. Students should be able to di-

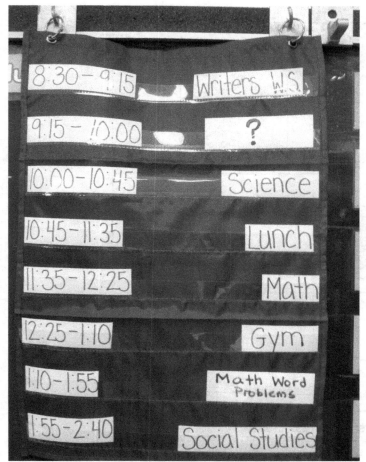

Figure 2.10. **Mystery schedule.**

Reading	📖
Math	$123^{+x}_{-÷}$
Speech with Ms. Jessica	
Art	🎨

Figure 2.11. **Individual mini-schedule.**

rectly interact with the mini-schedule (e.g., remove or flip over the picture/written text of each activity or cross off each activity after it is completed); encourage students to refer to their schedules frequently throughout the day. In the near term, this visual support can help organize students so that they know the different activities that make up their day, increasing predictability and comfort. In the long term, mini-schedules can help students develop both independence and self-monitoring skills.

Task-sequencing boards. A type of mini-schedule that breaks down an activity into its component parts or into a sequence of steps, task-sequencing boards are used with students who need additional visual support to complete certain tasks that are challenging for them. These boards give students written directions or pictorial representations of each step, which they are then to check off as it is completed. See Figure 2.12 for a sample.

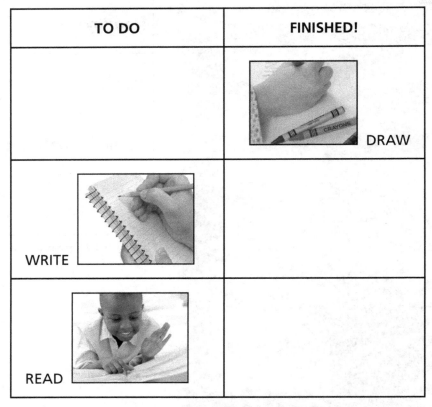

Figure 2.12. Task board.

This strategy is particularly useful for students who have difficulty sustaining attention during longer activities, those who have difficulty completing multistep activities, and students who find certain activities overwhelming or distressing. As students become older, they can begin to write their own task sequence with the guidance of a teacher, increasing their feelings of both competence and independence. Examples are shown in Figures 2.13, 2.14, and 2.15.

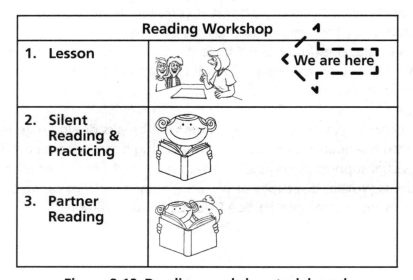

Figure 2.13. Reading workshop task board.

My Job in Writing Today!

☐ Write 1 topic sentence

☐ Write 3 supporting sentences

☐ Write 1 concluding sentence

☐ Edit paragraph

FINISHED? I can: <u>freewrite</u>

Figure 2.14. Writing workshop task board.

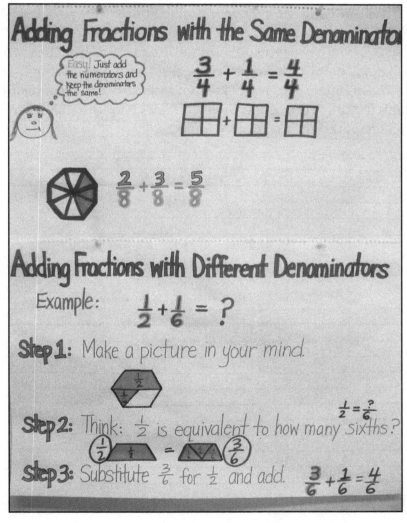

Figure 2.15. Adding fractions charts.

Visual aids to supplement verbal directions. Visual aids can be used in the place of as well as a supplement to verbal communication. For students with ASD, who are often better at visual than auditory processing, the use of visual aids such as pictures, words, drawings, or actual objects to accompany verbal instructions can help diminish uncertainty and prevent frustration that can lead to interfering behavior.

Some behavior that may appear to reflect noncompliance is actually a reflection of lack of understanding or confusion about what is expected or how to carry out a task For example, many teachers cite students' "calling out" as a common behavior problem in their classrooms. A two-sided card showing a student raising his hand on one side and a student raising his hand with an "X" over it on the other is a simple, easy visual to use to supplement verbal directions. At the start of a math lesson, the card can be turned to "raise your hand" as the teacher says, "Remember, in math we …" and points to the visual reminder. When it is time to move on to group discussion about the read-aloud, the teacher can flip the card to "do not raise your hand," thus clarifying the change in expectations.

Individuals with ASD often have difficulty with abstract concepts; thus, providing concrete examples and visual aids helps reduce ambiguity and clarify expectations. Examples of some additional visual aids utilized in ASD Nest Program include break cards (Figure 2.16), "When I Am Finished" visuals (Figure 2.17), center time schedules (Figure 2.18), partner job charts (Figure 2.19), and reading workshop directions (Figure 2.20).

Break Card

1. Move to the break area

2. Set the timer

3. Take a break

4. When time is up, rejoin the group!

***Figure 2.16.* Break card.**

Figure 2.17. "When I am finished" visual.

Figure 2.18. Center time schedule.

Figure 2.19. Partner jobs chart.

Reading Workshop

Today's Directions:

1. Fill out reading log

2. Read & think about characters' traits

3. Jot down one trait for each character

4. Complete reading log

Figure 2.20. Reading workshop directions.

The Incredible 5-Point Scale (Buron & Curtis, 2012). This visual scale can be used to illustrate a range of behaviors appropriate in various settings and activities. It should be clearly displayed for easy viewing and reference by students. Among other things, it should be used to teach voice modulation in all classrooms where voice volume levels impede concentration on learning tasks or make the room uncomfortable for students with auditory hypersensitivity. Use of this scale can also help elicit more audible voice levels from children who can barely be heard even in one-to-one settings. See Figure 2.21 for a sample Incredible 5-Point Voice Scale.

When teaching younger students the meaning and function of this scale, it is important to involve a high level of student-teacher interaction, using modeling by both students and teachers, game-like listening activities, and student role-play.

5	 😲	**Screaming/ Emergency**
4	 😛	**Recess/ Outside**
3	 😄	**Classroom Voice/ Talking**
2	 😮	**Soft Voice/ Whisper**
1	 🙂	**No Talking**

Figure 2.21. **The Incredible 5-Point voice scale.**

Voice modulation is one form of self-regulation. It applies not only to students but also to teachers. Very loud teacher voices can be overwhelming and frightening to children with ASD and should be restricted to the uses indicated by the Incredible 5-Point Scale. Displaying and teaching this scale helps teachers become more aware of their own voice volume. The Incredible 5-Point Scale can also be used to address various aspects of emotional control. See Figure 2.42 for an example of an Incredible 5-Point Control Scale.

Additional Strategies to Prevent Escalation of Problem Behavior

Modeling with self-talk. In this strategy, the teacher verbalizes her problem-solving method step-by-step, talking through her thinking process and presenting ways to resolve rather than exacerbate problem situations. The teacher verbally . . .

1. identifies a problem situation ("I want that game, but Michael has it.");

2. identifies the action a child may want to engage in and its likely outcome ("I want to take that game from Michael, but that will make him angry.");

3. considers other alternatives and their likely outcomes ("I could ask him if I can use the game with him or if we could trade games; maybe he will say yes."); and

4. comes to a decision ("I will ask Michael if he wants to trade games. If he says no, I will ask him if I can play that game with him").

Most of the following strategies are adapted from Myles and Southwick (2005):

- *Proximity control:* Move near the child who seems distressed rather than calling attention to signs of anxiety or frustration prior to escalation of impeding behavior (e.g., circulating around the room during a lesson, moving near the child who seems distressed or agitated prior to escalation of behavior).

- *Signal interference:* Use a nonverbal signal to let the child know you are aware of her difficulty/feelings of frustration (e.g., walk by the student, tap on her desk, or give a wink, nod, or secret signal chosen by the child ahead of time).

- *Distraction:* Shift the child's attention away from the distressing task or situation to quickly diffuse early stages of problem behavior (e.g., use humor, a topic of interest, or a brief interruption of an activity to sing a song, play a quick game, move around the room, or do a brief relaxation exercise).

- *"Looking forward to ..." approach:* Use an upcoming preferred activity to help the child focus on the current activity (e.g., reminding the child that it will be snack time right after the current disliked activity).

- *Antiseptic bouncing:* Remove the child from a distressing/overwhelming situation in a non-punitive way (e.g., send the child on a errand to the office, ask the child to drop off a book at another Nest classroom).

- *"Just walk, don't talk:"* Take a child who is displaying early signs of distress and difficulty maintaining self-regulation for a walk. Don't attempt to discuss the situation or be confrontational during this walk; the child should be free to say anything he wishes without fear of contradiction. Discussion/analysis of the situation should be dealt with through planned intervention after the distress has subsided.

Instructional Strategies and Supports

This section focuses on prevention through the use of strategies designed to (a) enable students to succeed at learning tasks; (b) give students a sense that their teachers care about them and their ideas; and (c) show students that their interests will be recognized and incorporated into the school experience. Communication plays a major role in achieving this. Clarity in teachers' communication is important. Positivity in teachers' communication is important. And listening to students and responding respectfully to their questions, concerns, requests, and desire to share experiences is important.

Basic Classroom Operation

Individuals with ASD tend to be literal, concrete thinkers, and often have difficulty with abstract concepts and inferential thinking. Therefore, using the following strategies when communicating with students with ASD can help to clarify expectations, reduce uncertainty and anxiety, and, ultimately, prevent interfering behavior.

Utilize positive behavioral instructions. Avoid using negatively phrased instructions (e.g., statements that include "don't," "stop," "no"). Upon hearing such directions, children may stop what they were doing or what they were about to do but not know what to do after that. Instead, whenever possible, use positively phrased statements to explain what to do. Telling students "what to do" helps to reduce uncertainty about what is expected and provides students with more concrete information.

Using visual supports, modeling, and/or prompting can bolster positive behavioral directives by providing students with an additional layer of support to reduce confusion or uncertainty that may lead to interfering behavior.

- Use clear, concise, developmentally appropriate language when providing instructions.
- Ensure the child understands what is expected and check for understanding.
- Provide "processing time" for verbally presented instructions.
- Use concrete examples when providing instructions, as children with ASD tend to learn better when concrete examples are used to illustrate abstract concepts. (For example, "Hang up your coat," rather than "Don't throw your coat on the floor.")

Provide opportunities for choice-making. Provide frequent opportunities for making choices throughout the day. This serves several purposes: (a) it gives students a feeling that they are active members of their classroom community, and thus the classroom is a place where they belong and want to be; (b) it helps create engagement in activities by enhancing motivation; and (c) it decreases noncompliance and other interfering behaviors (Bambara, Koger, Katzer, & Davenport, 1995; Shogren, Faggella-Luby, Bae, & Wehmeyer, 2004). The choices can be as simple as choosing where to sit at lunch, which of two songs the class should sing first, whether to use crayons or markers during a particular activity, and which of two activities the child would engage in when she has finished an assigned task. Examples of choice boards are shown in Figures 2.22, 2.23, and 2.24.

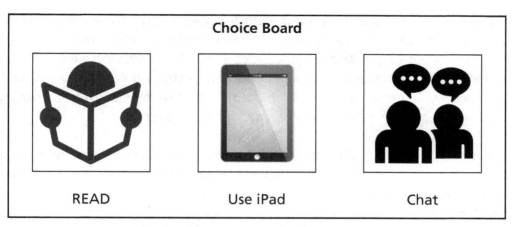

Figure 2.22. **Activity choice board.**

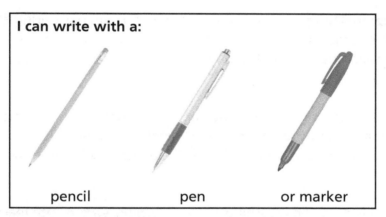

Figure 2.23. **Writing options choice board.**

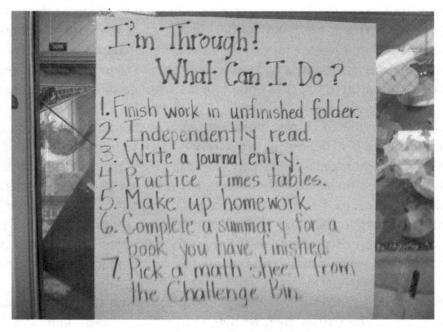

Figure 2.24. **"I'm through – what can I do?" chart.**

Priming. Priming is a process of preparing a student or students for a new learning experience in advance of its formal presentation or actual implementation (Koegel, Koegel, Frea, & Green-Hopkins, 2003; Wilde, Koegel, & Koegel, 1992). It involves previewing learning materials and learning activities under relaxed conditions, usually on a one-to-one basis, sometimes presenting new learning tasks in a simplified or more game-like format. Priming may be implemented by a teacher, a related service provider, or a parent.

Priming is particularly effective with students who need more time to learn new concepts and procedures as well as students with high anxiety levels for whom group instruction of new and challenging learning experiences is overwhelming. Group priming may be used for class experiences such as trips or assembly programs that are not only new but may introduce experiences and expectations that students find difficult or frightening.

Instructional grouping. Using a variety of instructional groupings during classroom activities facilitates delivering targeted, efficient instruction. Co-teaching models and small-group instruction can help tailor instruction to the needs of the students, thereby maximizing instructional time during lesson.

Different models of integrative co-teaching can help educators differentiate for a variety of student learning styles and academic readiness levels, while also decreasing the number of students in each lesson. Friend and Cook (2012) outlined six co-teaching models, shown in Figure 2.25.

The more traditional format of co-teaching is *team teaching*, where both teachers are in front of the class and take active roles in the delivery of instruction during the lesson. The teachers may take turns addressing the students or use role-play, with one teaching and the other modeling what the students are going to be doing. Other models of co-teaching include one *teach, one observe*, where one teacher leads the lesson while the other circulates around the class collecting data on students and *one teach, one assist* model, where one teacher leads the lesson while the other teachers circulates around the class and provides supports to individual students.

The three remaining models of co-teaching each involves breaking up the class into smaller groups for more targeted instruction. In the *parallel teaching model*, the class is split into two groups, and the two teachers deliver instruction to their own groups at the same time. Groups are flexible, divided based on skill level, interests, learning styles, or other criteria. Groups are changed frequently to ensure that both teachers get the opportunity to work with all of their students. In the *alternative teaching* model, one teacher takes responsibility for teaching the lesson to larger group of students, while the other teacher works with a smaller group to teach missed content, review challenging concepts, or introduce more advanced material.

The last model is *station teaching*. Although requiring some classroom management and planning, this model can be extremely effective. In the station teaching model, teachers break content into at least two parts, and students cycle through stations learning the different content. With more than two stations, the students work in some stations independently while the teachers facilitate the other groups.

Co-teachers use the six different co-teaching models based on the needs of their students and the content that is being delivered. By modifying the format of the lessons, teachers can work to meet the needs of all of their students and provide the necessary learning environment and support.

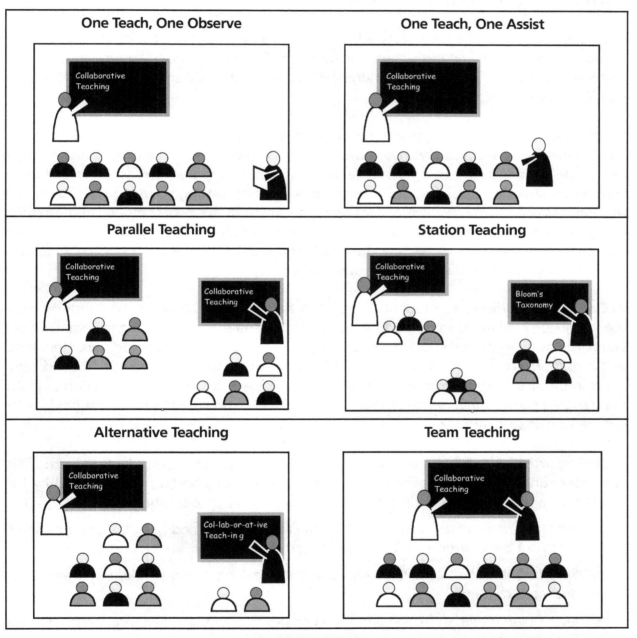

***Figure 2.25.* Friend's co-teaching models.**

(Based on the work of Friend & Cook, 2012; icons created by A. Lanou, 2005.)

Small-group activities. Small-group activities following lessons can provide struggling students opportunities to receive additional support or students who are ready to be challenged opportunities to receive more advanced content. It is important to vary the co-teaching models used to match the needs of the students and the content. In addition, the students in various small groups should be changed regularly to ensure that they get the opportunity to work in different groups. In the ASD Nest Program, both the special and general education teacher are trained and expected to work with *all* students in their class across all subject areas, which makes this instructional flexibility possible.

Peer-based supports. These supports, which include various types of peer buddies, peer mentoring, and peer-mediated instruction, can be quite effective in enhancing social interactions and fostering relationships among children with ASD and their classmates (Owen-DeSchryver, Carr, Cale, Blakeley-Smith, 2008).

To set up peer-based support, first, identify peers who display mutual interest in each other, making sure that the typical child demonstrates a helping disposition. Second, facilitate a peer mentoring relationship in two ways by (a) providing more opportunities for the children involved to interact (e.g., seating them next to one another, putting them together for paired reading, making them line partners, assigning them jointly to classroom jobs and errands); and (b) providing either formal training or informal guidance to the typical peer mentor on how to be most useful to his partner. Some children with ASD can also serve as peer mentors in specific situations with appropriate guidance.

Activity/task modifications. Students in the ASD Nest Program participate in inclusion classrooms and are held to the same grade-level academic standards, outlined in the Common Core Standards, as their general education peers. (For information on the Common Core Standards, visit http://www.corestandards.org/.) Similar to many other students with special needs, students in the ASD Nest program may benefit from some activity or task modification to make the standard curriculum more accessible. Such accommodations and/or modifications may be outlined in the student's IEP.

Modifying activities, tasks, and/or materials is an effective way to help students to learn while also preventing problem behavior triggered by task difficulty and/or duration, and by the heightened anxiety that engenders. Examples of task modifications include:

- *Reteach or review the lesson* on which the task is based, modifying the presentation if it has not been sufficiently effective for particular children.

- *Simplify the task or activity* by shortening it, breaking it into smaller steps, and/or reducing its duration.

- *Modify the materials* involved in a task or provide a variety of appropriate materials (e.g., different types of paper and writing utensils) to allow the child to use those with which she feels most comfortable. Individual organization systems can also be used.

- *Encourage communication* from the child on the difficulty being experienced.

- *Increase assistance* to the child during the task or activity so as to support good performance and reduce the child's anxiety about completing the task correctly. (Don't wait until the child has made errors or her anxiety has escalated to the point where it impedes performance.)

- *Provide frequent opportunities* to take breaks or move around the classroom during a challenging task.

Homework

Task modification is often particularly important with regard to homework assignments. Many parents of students with ASD report struggles with their children over the completion of challenging homework assignments in academic areas. Such situations may be significantly reduced by using strategies as simple as treating homework as a way of reviewing or reinforcing work already completed in class or substantially reducing the number of math examples to be done at home.

Incorporate students' interests. Many students with ASD have a particular area of special or intense interest (e.g., trains, cartoons, movie characters). In order to enhance motivation and encourage active participation in activities (in particular, more difficult tasks), try to incorporate students' particular interests into lessons, activities, and tasks. For example, creating math worksheets that include trains, if that's a special interest, or reading a story about a student's special interest area. Incorporating students' special interests can build a positive rapport with the students, further increasing the likelihood that they will be motivated to engage in class. Examples of ways to incorporate students' interests are shown in Figures 2.26, 2.27, and 2.28. See also Power Cards on pages 47-48.

Figure 2.26. Reminder to wear your glasses cue card.

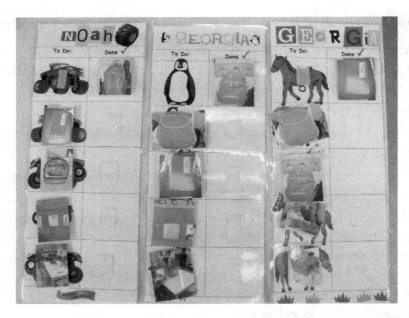

Figure 2.27. Individualized interest-based visual cues for unpacking.

Figure 2.28. Cookie in/out boxes – an interest-based visual for math.

Provide support during transitions. Transitions between settings and/or activities have been found to be challenging for many individuals with ASD due to a lack of predictability associated with the nature of transition routines (Sterling-Turner & Jordan, 2007). For example, many students experience difficulty ending an activity they are engaged in prior to the transition or are unclear about what is expected or what to do during the transition itself.

A number of strategies have been found to be extremely effective in enhancing predictability and reducing interfering behavior correlated with transition difficulty.

- *High-probability requests* are based on the concept of behavioral momentum. They involve presenting the student with three to five requests to perform a skill that is both simple and motivating right before presenting her with a less preferred activity or a more challenging task. This strategy provides the child with opportunities to experience success, enhances motivation, and can decrease the likelihood that problem behavior will occur (Banda & Kubina, 2006).

  For lower grades, the teacher could lead the class in a quick game of "following the leader" while transitioning from the classroom to the lunchroom; for example, presenting directions for a series of simple gross-motor movement that the students must imitate (e.g., "touch your feet, give your partner a high-five, place your hands at your side, and quietly walk in the line to lunch"). For upper grades, prior to transitioning to a more challenging math task, the teacher could lead the class in some basic math fact drills, allowing the students to feel successful going into the more demanding lesson.

- *Visual supports* such as "First … Then" boards (see Figure 2.29), mini-schedules, or checklists have been found to be highly effective in increasing the speed and success of transitions both within the steps of an activity as well as between different activities (Dettmer et al., 2000). Visual supports provide the student with increased structure and predictability, making the routine less overwhelming and easier to complete. Depicting the sequence of steps involved in the routine helps to make the transition more concrete, as the student is provided with a clearer understanding of what to expect.

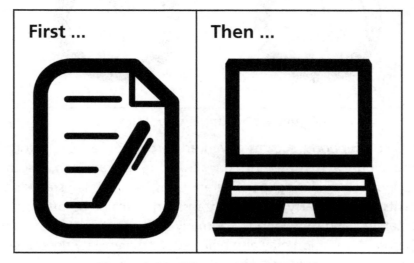

Figure 2.29. "First … then" board.

- *Peer supports* may be useful in helping children more successfully negotiate transitions. For example, a peer buddy may assist a child who is confused by modeling the expected behavior and encouraging that child to engage in the next activity with him or her.

- *Timers* (see, for example, www.timetimer.com), a specific type of visuals, can be helpful for students who have difficulty with transitions. Timers signal the end of an activity (e.g., five minutes before it is time to clean up and sit on the rug) or remind students of the amount of time remaining in an activity (e.g., three minutes left in a break before having to return to the group). See Figure 2.30 for a sample timer.

This strategy helps students prepare themselves for transitions, providing additional structure to assist them in organizing their time during challenging activities.

Note

Some students with ASD fixate on timers; for such students the use of timers should be closely monitored to avoid initiating or intensifying such fixation. Also, auditory timers are frightening to some young children with ASD who have strong auditory sensitivities or are highly anxious. For such children, visual timers serve as a useful alternative.

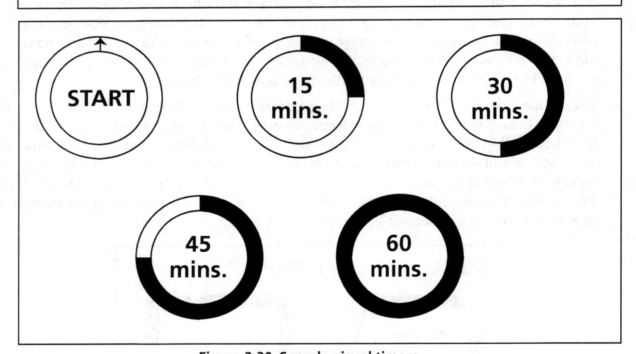

Figure 2.30. Sample visual timers.

- *Additional transition supports,* such as advanced verbal notice (e.g., "Stop, look, listen – you have three more minutes …"), transition songs that outline transition expectation (e.g., "clean-up" songs), or songs played during specific transitions, can help to establish a more predictable routine. Students can also carry preferred transition items or be offered choices to increase comfort, predictability, and motivation. For many students, a couple of minutes of relaxation exercises just before a transition may also help reduce the anxiety generated by change to another environment or challenging activity.

Social Supports That Strengthen Social Relational Development and Social Cognition

In the Nest Program, social strategies are incorporated throughout the school day, aimed at addressing the core social challenges of students with ASD. There are six areas of social supports: Experience sharing, language and dynamic communication, social problem solving, social cognition, flexibility, and using strengths and preferred interests.

Sharing Experiences

Social supports in the classroom are designed to promote true engagement and interaction, as well as to highlight shared experiences between classmates. Students learn to gather and share information in dynamic learning exchanges.

Labeling the moment. Brainstorm a word or phrase together to capture a moment. (After a group puzzle activity, label the memory as *"The Puzzling Puzzle Search."*)

Declarative language. Invite students to interact by sharing thoughts, making comments, and wondering. See Figure 2.31 for examples.

What might declarative language sound like?

Wondering: "I wonder why this character would ..."

Inviting: "Let's try to solve this without calculators."

Self-narrating: "I'm going to go back to the text ..."

Commenting: "I didn't think the story would go in *this* direction!"

Figure 2.31. **Examples of declarative language.**

Language and Dynamic Communication

Expressive, receptive, and pragmatic language challenges can impact students' ability to succeed in their school environment. It is important for educators to consider both *their own* language and their *students'* language needs.

Wait time. Provide ample time for the child to process language. Some students need additional time to process language.

"Checking in." Eliminate the expectation of sustained eye contact. Direct eye contact is uncomfortable for many students with ASD and can interfere with processing language. Encourage the concept of "checking in" rather than requiring a student to "look at me." This builds an understanding of an important nonverbal expectation of the speaker. Some examples of "checking-in" language are listed in Figure 2.32.

> **Encouraging checking in might sound like this:**
>
> "Alex, thanks for **checking in** with me with your eyes.
>
> I was not sure you heard my directions,
>
> but you looked up at me and so *now* I *know* you heard me."

Figure 2.32. Examples of "checking-in" language.

Social Problem Solving

Problem solving requires recognition of the problem, involves consideration of multiple solutions, and demands novel thinking. A positive spin on problem solving demystifies the process and makes searching for solutions both an enjoyable and attainable challenge. For example, rather than drawing attention to the negative, "Oh no, you have a problem; your marker box is missing the red marker!," a kindergarten teacher might say, "Class, Robyn has a problem to solve! We're *great* at solving problems in K-301! Let's see how she's thinking of solving this ..."

Size of the problem. Five-point problem scales (see page 47) can help distinguish a big problem from a little problem. Many students on the autism spectrum become overwhelmed by routine problems such as misplacing their pencil and may have trouble thinking through how to handle such situations.

Also, a chart such as the following can be effective:

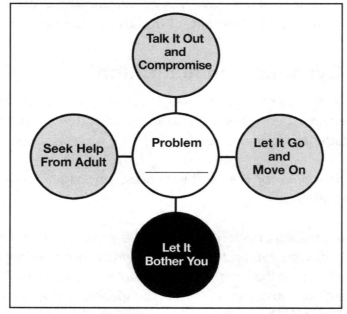

From Mataya, K. *Successful Problem-Solving for High-Functioning Students With Autism Spectrum Disorders*, 2013 (p. 6). Shawnee Mission, KS: AAPC Publishing. Used with permission.

Learning to differentiate between big and little problems can help students start to recognize that they can be problem solvers. A teacher might coach, "You can't find your pencil? Oh, that seems like a little problem we've solved before pretty easily. I'm thinking back, now what did we do last time we had this little problem …" This approach invites students to reflect back on solutions they may have came up with in the past and helps them monitor their level of frustration. The teacher can coach the student through considering the size of the current problem (can it be solved fairly easily? Quickly? Independently?). However, it is important not to tell students how *they* are feeling about a particular problem. For example, if a student says that losing his pencil is a big problem, teachers may support him in solving the problem and then, after the problem is solved, begin to highlight, "Hey, that problem *felt* big to you, but I'm thinking *now* that it was pretty easy to solve and we solved it pretty quickly! Maybe next time it might feel like a smaller problem!"

Roles. The use of roles helps students recognize their place in a group and promotes group problem solving (e.g., one person can be the director, one can be the reporter, and a third can be the camera person). Figure 2.33 shows how roles can be used in third-grade math groups working on problem solving, showing their thinking.

Using Roles to Support Math Word Problem Group Work
(4-person math groups)

Team Math Challenge:
Work together to solve the following math problem! Each person on the team needs to take on a ROLE to help the group complete this challenge.

Omer looked out of his window during breakfast on Sunday morning and saw pigeons and dogs passing by. He counted all the legs of the pigeons and dogs and found that the total number of legs added up to 66. How many of each kind of animal (pigeons and dogs) passed by his window if the total number of animals was 24?

Role 1: **Artist** – draw out the problem and the team's thinking

Role 2: **Planner** – listen to everyone's ideas and help the team write out the plan (including a number sentence)

Role 3: **Calculator** – help the team do the calculation to solve the problem to get to a final answer

Role 4: **Writer** – write out how your team solved this problem in complete sentences

---

Figure 2.33. Language of roles.

Social Cognition

Social cognition involves thinking about the dynamic social world (Aarts, 2012). In the younger grades (K-2), we work on developing an understanding of the social concepts through highlighting and modeling. These concepts are more directly explored in the older grades.

Social clues. Explore social clues such as facial expressions, gestures, verbal and nonverbal language, environment, and context. For example, playing games of charades can encourage students to use clues to guess feelings, such as "excited," "nervous," or "scared," or actions, such as "reading," "playing basketball," or "blowing out birthday candles." Simple nonverbal scenes can also be acted out, such as the teacher looking at his watch, then at the door, and then at the clock before rolling his eyes. The students can try to guess what that teacher might be thinking or feeling based on nonverbal and context clues. Activities such as these help students explore recognizing and interpreting social clues in their environments.

Social Thinking® and social cognitive vocabulary. Specific language is used in the classroom to highlight social concepts and help increase students' awareness and understanding of the social world of school. Using Social Thinking® vocabulary such as Michelle Garcia Winner's "people files©" and "making a smart guess©" can help students think about what they know about their classmates and also use this information to make inferences about them (Winner, 2005).

Teachers can use additional social cognitive language such as "thinking together" and "our body sends a message" to help students understand what it takes to learn together with their classmates in a shared classroom. Such social cognitive language can help to promote generalization of the underlying social concepts across the students' school day. See Figure 2.34 for examples of social cognitive vocabulary used in the ASD Nest Program classrooms.

Social Vocabulary in the Classroom

"Wow! That was a **smart guess®**! (Winner, 2005) You used the information about the character in order to ..."

"When we connect all of your answers, I see that the class is **thinking together,** so ..."

"You both thought to write a story about footprints on the moon. Cool, **brain match!**"

Figure 2.34. **Examples of social cognitive vocabulary in ASD Nest program classrooms.**

Flexibility

Students on the spectrum prefer routines and sameness and tend to struggle with change and unpredictability (Sterling-Turner & Jordan, 2007).

"Flexibility" language. Highlight the concept of flexibility in the classroom (e.g., "You were flexible when you decided to use a different color when there were no blue markers left" or "I wonder if we can all think flexibly and imagine what it would be like to be a child in Colonial America; many things would be different.").

Partnerships. Tasks that require collaboration can help students problem solve and think flexibly as a team. For example, a fourth-grade teacher can set up math partnerships in her class. Each partnership might be challenged to work as a team to solve a problem such as, "How can you figure out the square footage of the classroom with nothing but a spool of yarn and a 12-inch ruler?" To come up with an answer, teams will have to think together, discussing each of their different plans and collaborating to reach a common goal. The teacher can circulate to support not only the mathematical concepts but also the strategies that help when working in a partnership.

"Good enough." This phrase highlights the fact that perfection is not always expected or attainable. A teacher might model this concept, sketching out an idea she has during writing workshop: "This is a sketch of my dog, because my story is going to be all about him. It doesn't look exactly like him, but it's good enough! It doesn't have to be perfect- this is just to help me plan the story I am going to write." Finding ways to integrate this concept of "good enough" can help increase students' flexibility and draw the focus away from rigid adherence to perfection.

Highlighting preferences. Discuss likes, dislikes, and personal preferences and emphasize that having different opinions is okay. Students may participate in a class survey of likes and dislikes, interviewing each other and tabulating the results. The teachers can highlight that different people have different preferences: "You LOVE Star Wars Legos®, but Anthony only thinks that they are O.K. That's alright; everyone has their own preferences!" Teachers may also unearth new connections students may have with one another, "Look, Anthony said that he HATES roller coasters, and so do you! You two are connected on that."

Using Strengths and Preferred Interests

Capitalizing on strengths and interests can tap into students' motivation and learning style. Figure 2.35 shows how one teacher encourages a student to share her strength in knowing her math facts with the whole class.

"Amelia, something I know about you is that you have an AMAZING memory for math facts! Did you know that lots of kids find learning their math facts really hard? This is a real strength of yours, and some of your classmates could really use your expertise. Maybe we could set up fact buddies, and you could help some of your classmates who are having a hard time learning their facts. I'm sure that they'd really appreciate your help.

Figure 2.35. **Example of celebrating strengths.**

Balancing discussions of strengths and challenges. Develop self-awareness of strengths and relative challenges. During a writing conference with a third-grade student, a teacher may have an open discussion with the student highlighting how her keen eye for detail makes her a great editor – her spelling and punctuation are almost perfect! The teacher can then lead the student to explore how sometimes going back and revising one's work can be hard. "I know that once you write a scene, you want it to be finished, and you do not like to go back and change things. Rewriting is also tough for you. These are two things we are going to work on as they can help you become a stronger writer. Let's talk about why revising might help you,..." Such open discussion can help students recognize that they, like everyone in their class, have both areas of strength and difficulty, and that is okay.

Matching interests/strengths to roles. Incorporate strengths and interests when defining roles to help students channel their intrinsic motivation towards working with their group. A student who is particularly strong in computation could be the group's "calculation's checker," providing him with a role within his math group. A student who is passionate about game shows can make a great announcer for a classroom spelling bee. Finding ways to incorporate students' interests and capitalize on their strengths helps build confidence in the classroom and also highlights different ways to be part of the class community.

Celebrating strengths to build competence. Helping students learn to recognize and celebrate their individual strengths can help increase their feelings of competence as well as their intrinsic motivation. For example, during morning meeting, students can go around and share one thing in which they feel that they *really* excel. Teachers can help to point out how some of the more unique interests of our students with ASD can be assets to the class community, "Alex knows *every* train line in New York City; he could be a great navigator when we go to the Bronx Zoo next month!"

Celebrating strengths can help build motivation for students who may struggle in the classroom. For a student who has difficulty with writing, for example, the teacher might share with the class, "You know, Halley knows how to draw every Pokémon character; I bet she could even create her own comic book for our classroom library. We could also make copies for other classes! Maybe someone wants to partner with her on this and be the writer so that she can be the illustrator?"

Social narratives. Social narratives, including Social Stories™ developed by Carol Gray (1994, 2010), is an empirically supported strategy used to help children develop a better understanding of social expectations and clarify ways to cope with challenging social situations. The underlying premise of this strategy is that once the social expectation of a particular environment is clarified, students can better negotiate the situation. Social narratives are written from the child's perspective, and typically describe the difficult situation, skill, or concept in terms of the relevant social cues, perspectives, and responses.

Social narratives are made up of different types of sentences, including *descriptive sentences* describing facts of the situation, *perspective sentences* highlighting the feelings and responses of the people involved, *cooperative sentences* sharing how others can help in the situation, *affirmative sentences* stating common values relevant to the situation, *control sentences* written by the child and identifying personal strategies, and *directive sentences* guiding student behavior. The ratio of sentences is one directive sentence for every two or more sentences of another type (perspective, cooperative, etc.). The teacher reads the story with the student on multiple occasions prior to the occurrence of the difficult situation, thereby enhancing predictability (Kokina & Kern, 2010). See Figure 2.36 for a sample kindergarten social narrative.

Sammy's Book About Going First
My name is Sammy, and I like to go first. Sometimes I get to go first, and I feel happy! Sometime *other* children go first. *Pg. 1*
Everyone has a place in line: Sometimes first, sometimes last, and sometimes in the middle. We all take turns! *Pg. 2*
Lots of my classmates really like to go first – just like me! *Sometimes not going first is hard.* *Pg. 3*
I can try to remember, **"Everyone gets a chance to go first, and going last or in the middle is okay!** I *will* **get to go first another time!"** *Pg. 4*

Figure 2.36. **Sample social narrative.**

Cartooning. Cartooning, including Comic Strip Conversations™, also developed by Carol Gray, uses a simple drawing to break down communicative exchanges between two or more people. As a visual strategy, illustrations help to clarify social interactions. Dialogue bubbles, thought bubbles, and different colors are used to represent what different people said and what they might have thought and felt during a social situation. This is also a helpful strategy for gaining insight into how the student on the spectrum may have interpreted a situation. Figure 2.37 depicts some of the common icons used in cartooning.

Cartooning may be used to highlight a positive social interaction, such as when a student on the spectrum helps a classmate. It may also be used to clarify a confusing social situation, such as why some people might want to play something different than you at recess. In addition, cartooning can be very helpful for breaking down a complex social situation to facilitate problem solving, thereby developing both perspective-taking and flexibility (Glaeser, Pierson, & Fritschman, 2003). The strategy can be used in the classroom, during lunch, or during recess. It can also be a powerful tool to support reading comprehension and other academic tasks.

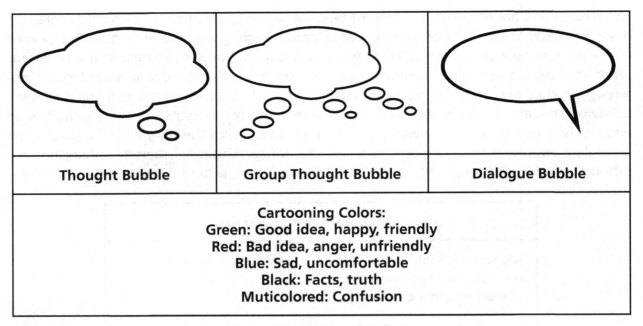

Thought Bubble	Group Thought Bubble	Dialogue Bubble

Cartooning Colors:
Green: Good idea, happy, friendly
Red: Bad idea, anger, unfriendly
Blue: Sad, uncomfortable
Black: Facts, truth
Muticolored: Confusion

Figure 2.37. Cartooning icons.

Role-play. Role-play can help a group of students explore social scenarios or help an individual child rehearse for an upcoming new or difficult situation. Teaching teams can model and highlight social concepts and problem solving by role-playing with one another. Alternatively, a teacher can model first, followed by role-playing with the students. For children with ASD, additional steps may be needed, such as role-play between one teacher and one typical child, between one or two teachers and a child with ASD, or between one or two typical children and a child with ASD.

Replacement Behavior

Replacement behavior refers to substituting appropriate and productive behavior for impeding/interfering behavior. The impeding behavior to be replaced may interfere with the individual student's learning, the learning of other students, and the child's acceptance by peers.

Functional Communication Training

This involves teaching the child ways to communicate wants, needs, dislikes, and preferences in more appropriate ways (Bambara & Kern, 2005; Carr & Durand, 1985). A functional behavior assessment (FBA) may be needed with some children to identify the function of the interfering behavior (Aspy & Grossman, 2011; Dunlap et al., 2010; O'Neill et al., 1997), but in other children, the function of the impeding behavior is clear without an FBA.

The replacement behavior should be something that (a) the child is capable of doing, (b) can be easily taught and used, and (c), most important, serves the same function as the problem behavior. Examples of replacement behaviors (alternative forms of communication) include teaching the child more appropriate ways to (a) request assistance when needed, (b) obtain attention from others, (c) request a break from overwhelming sensory situations or very difficult work, or (d) request a desired object or activity.

Functional communication training is part of communication skill development. Examples include the following:

HELP cards. Teaching children to use a HELP card when a task is very difficult for them to deal with independently can prevent the heightened stress that often precedes a "meltdown." This strategy involves teaching students to recognize when their distress level is escalating because of an inability to carry out an assigned task independently and then selecting an response, which may be done by use of the HELP card (shown in Figure 2.38). This strategy is only effective if the HELP card results in a response to the child's communication within a short time. (Under some circumstances, the HELP card may first bring assistance from a peer mentor.)

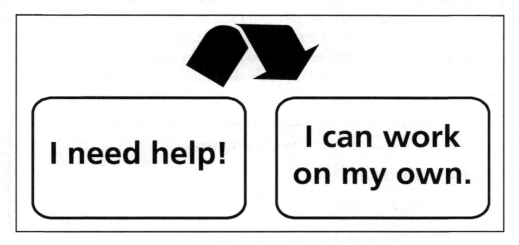

Figure 2.38. HELP card.

"Break" program. This strategy involves teaching students to self-monitor to identify feelings of anxiety and distress, and subsequently replace interfering behavior with a more appropriate method of coping. A designated "calming corner" (quiet, set-off area) should be used as a break area where students can relax/self-soothe when needed. A variety of relaxation tools such as koosh balls, stress balls, headphones, or a CD player with calming music should be kept in the calming corner for students to use while on their break.

As part of the program, students are taught to request a break when they become overwhelmed or distressed during an activity/situation. A "break card" may be used as a visual cue to help prompt students to request the break. In teaching children this replacement behavior, teachers may prompt the student to hold up the break card (request a break) and go to the calming corner at the first sign that the child's distress is escalating, threatening to precipitate a "meltdown." The teacher then sets a timer for 3-5 minutes (exact time is determined by the amount of time the student has needed in the past to recharge and rejoin the group) and encourages the student to use one or more of the relaxation tools available. Once the timer beeps, the teacher prompts the student to return to the previous activity.

The ultimate goal of this program is for the child to learn to self-monitor and spontaneously request and implement breaks independently as needed. It is important that teachers distinguish breaks from rewards or free time, as this strategy is intended to be used as a *coping* skill to replace problem behavior, not a form of positive reinforcement.

Enhancing Self-Management

The strategies in this category involve teaching the student more appropriate and effective ways to cope with distress, anxiety, fear, and anger.

Deep breathing exercises and progressive muscle relaxation training. These techniques can be introduced by the occupational therapist and used by the entire class (with practice). Individual children can receive additional training in how to implement the strategies when they experience distress or feel overwhelmed as a way to replace challenging behavior (Cautela & Groden, 1978; Mullins & Christian, 2001). A sample visual cue depicting "cool-down steps" is shown in Figure 2.39.

Steps to COOL down ...

1. Ask for a **BREAK**

2. Take **3 DEEP** breaths

3. Count to **10** *slowly* **1-2-3-** ...

Are you calm and ready to come back?

Figure 2.39. Steps to cool down cue card.

School-based yoga. Yoga for the social setting can be introduced by the occupational therapist and can include a series of poses and postures beneficial for increasing body awareness, self-regulation, as well as breathing exercises and relaxation techniques for calming and improved concentration (Stück & Gloeckner, 2005). Yoga can be used as a therapeutic intervention for the whole classroom, small groups, or individual students.

Problem-solving frameworks. Students on the spectrum can have difficulty identifying a problem, recognizing its cause(s), coming up with one or more solutions, and then evaluating the selected solution to plan for addressing this problem in the future.

Problem-solving frameworks can help students recognize the components of problem solving, break down the steps to address a problem, and organize their response. For younger students, teachers first model the problem-solving process using self-talk. A problem-solving song, like the one shown in Figure 2.40, can make the process more fun and manageable. An entire class can help an individual student recognize and solve problems, or individual students can remind themselves of the steps with the lyrics of an easily remembered song.

Problem Solving Song!
(Sung to the tune of "It's Raining, It's Pouring")

A *problem!* A *problem!*
When you have a *problem* ...
Think about it,
Get ideas,
Choose the best solution!

Figure 2.40. **Problem-solving song.**

For older students, more advanced problem-solving frameworks may be used. For example, Situation, Options, Consequences, Choice, Strategy, and Simulation or "S.O.C.C.S.S." (Roosa, cited in Myles & Southwick, 2005) can be a powerful tool for more advanced students who need support in recognizing the cause of a problem, considering the possible consequences of various solutions, preparing for the solution they would like to try, and reflecting on their solution to help them better plan for the future. With the initial support of an adult, students complete a S.O.C.C.S.S. sheet (see Figure 2.41), selecting and rehearsing a solution with desired consequences, and returning later to evaluate their choices. This strategy empowers students to consider the ramifications of their actions while also helping them to organize their thinking.

Two other problem-solving strategies are also used in the ASD Nest model – social autopsies and Social Behavior Mapping© (Winner, 2005). Both are used after a social problem has occurred. In social autopsies, the child and an adult facilitator explore a "social error" that the child made, discussing the error itself and its impact and then quickly moving to developing a plan to avoid that error in the future (Myles & Southwick, 2005). In Social Behavior Mapping©, the adult helps the child think through various actions that were taken and should have been taken, recording on a chart how those different behaviors might make *others* feel as well as how they make the *student him/herself* feel. The consequences that the student would experience for displaying the "correct" and the "problematic" behaviors are also noted. These problem-solving strategies are geared toward helping students learn to understand and better navigate social difficulties, thereby setting them up to be more successful problem solvers in the future.

SITUATION:

Who was there?: _____

What happened (problem)?: _____

Where?: _____ *When?:* _____

Why?: _____

OPTIONS	**C**ONSEQUENCES / RESULTS	**C**hoice

STRATEGY – Plan of action

SIMULATION (Select one)
For whatever simulation you choose, think about
- What might others do, think, feel?
- What might you do, think, or feel?
- Does this still seem like the best option?
- Think about short and long-term consequences

1. Act out your option(s)	
2. Draw / write out option(s)	
3. Stop and think about option(s)- make a picture / mind movie	
4. _____	

Simulation outcomes, notes, or reminders:

Figure 2.41. S.O.C.C.S.S. chart.

(Adapted from Myles & Southwick, 2005.)

The Incredible 5-Point Control Scales. Five-point scales can be used to help students develop self-management skills (Buron & Curtis, 2012). Many students on the spectrum seem to go from "0 to 60" without recognizing that they are becoming upset or anxious. Five-point scales like that shown in Figure 2.42 ranking levels of control can help students become more aware of their escalating feelings.

Teachers and therapists, such as occupational therapists, can help students recognize the levels where they are on their "control scales." A student who feels "content" at level 1 can begin to recognize that she may begin to feel "hot" and "nervous" when she is at level 2 and that she may need to take some deep breaths to regain control. That same student can also learn that when she feels like she is at level 5, her body is "not in control" and a break may be necessary.

5	I NEED TO LEAVE!
4	I need some space.
3	Please don't talk.
2	I am a *little* nervous/ uncomfortable
1	I can handle this.

Figure 2.42. **Sample levels of control scale.**

Power Cards. Power Cards (Gagnon, 2001) can be excellent tools for helping students learn and practice coping strategies by incorporating their preferred interests (Keeling, Myles, Gagnon, & Simpson, 2003). Power Cards consist of a script, outlining how a favorite character or celebrity has challenges similar to those faced by the student and how they try to handle these shared difficulties. Especially in the beginning, the student may read the script daily or even multiple times a day to gain familiarity and comfort. A smaller, abbreviated Power Card version of the script featuring an image of the preferred character is also created that the student can keep in her desk, pocket, or book bag for quick reference, when needed. Two sample Power Cards, one for a kindergartener and one for fifth-grader are shown in Figure 2.43.

Timmy is very fast, and he does not like other trains to go faster than him. Sometimes he rushes and misses his stops or blows his engine. Oh no! Timmy likes to go fast, but he reminds himself to SLOW DOWN. When Timmy needs to slow down his engine, he tries to:

1. Take 16 deep breaths

2. Count back from 20

3. Say, "I can slooooooooow down."

Thor is a powerful hero and a protector of mankind who can sometimes lose control. Thor wants YOU to try to remember 3 things to help catch yourself before you react:

1. Tell the person bothering you, "Stop!"

2. Take 5 deep breaths

3. Walk away and ask a teacher for help

Figure 2.43. **Sample Power Cards.**

Video modeling. Video modeling taps into the visual preferences of students with ASD. This technique involves capturing scenarios, interactions, and activities on video, (minimally) editing the video to show positive experiences, and then showing the video to a student/students to teach and/or enhance a particular skill or set of skills (Bellini & Akullian, 2007; Shukla-Mehta, Miller, & Callahan, 2010). The videos may show adults, slightly older children, or the child himself (*video self-modeling*).

For example, one ASD Nest kindergarten class watched a videotape of a staged fire drill with students in a second-grade ASD Nest class modeling the procedure. The second graders showed what it looked like to listen to their teacher, line up with their partners quickly and quietly, and walk through the hallway. The kindergarten students watched the video, discussed what they observed, and practiced the behaviors they had seen. At the next fire drill, the kindergarten class was much better able to follow the procedures that had been modeled.

Positive Reinforcement Systems

This evidence-based practice involves modifying the ways in which teachers and others who interact and work with a child respond to both problematic behaviors (decreasing the likelihood that they will be displayed) and positive/replacement behaviors (to increase the likelihood that they will be used consistently in the future). Our goal is to always take advantage of the power of positive reinforcement.

Reinforcement systems, in a variety of formats, can be implemented on a classroom-wide level or on an individual basis (Scheuermann, 2012). The basic premise underlying these systems involves providing the student with a "reward" upon the performance of a certain skill or task, or for displaying (not displaying) a specific behavior, with the ultimate goal of increasing the likelihood that the behavior/skill will be used in the future.

General Practices

"Catch children being good!" This positive-reinforcement-based technique essentially involves providing increased positive attention and specific praise generously throughout the day each time a student displays a desired behavior or attempts to engage in a more appropriate behavior (Marcus & Vollmer, 1996). When providing reinforcement, it is important to specify what the child did to elicit positive feedback in order to increase the likelihood that she will use this skill/behavior again in the future (e.g., "I like the way you used your words to tell us what upset you."). For more examples, see Figure 2.44.

Figure 2.44. **Examples of "catching them being good!" phrases.**

The "catch them being good" technique increases attention being paid to positive behavior while reducing the focus on the negative or undesired behavior, in order to reduce the likelihood that it will be displayed. For more alternatives to attending to negative behavior, see Figure 2.45.

Instead of attending to a negative behavior, you could:

- Highlight and compliment students who are doing the "right thing"
- Restate the expectations and why you have them
- Compliment a student who is starting to do the "right thing"
- Use the "looking forward to approach" (see page 25) and highlight an upcoming preferred activity to motivate behavior change

---

Figure 2.45. **Alternatives to attending to undesirable behavior.**

Some children enjoy very demonstrative modes of reinforcement while others can only tolerate quiet displays of recognition, so care should be taken to match the type and level of reinforcement to the individual pattern of the child.

Reduce direct attention provided to interfering behaviors. Essentially, using this strategy, when the child engages in problem behavior, the adult limits the amount of attention provided. For example, the adult does not intentionally make eye contact with the child nor verbally comment on the behavior (e.g., the adult does not tell the child "stop it" or "don't do that") because any form of attention, which is what the child may be seeking, will only further reinforce the negative behavior.

It is important to remember that during instances of problematic behavior, a child is usually not receptive to learning a new skill, nor is he likely to comprehend why he should not be engaging in the interfering behavior; hence, this is not a teachable moment (Myles & Southwick, 2005).

Classwide Reinforcement Systems

Any classroom management system should be aligned with the overall philosophy and systems utilized by the school. In the ASD Nest Program, the systems we recommend are all based on principles of positive reinforcement, as the research clearly demonstrates the effectiveness of reward-based procedures (Horner et al., 1990). We caution against the use of any system that relies on punishment-based procedures (e.g., taking away points or privileges), as there is ample research evidence suggesting that such strategies are not effective in bringing about meaningful and lasting behavior change (Matson & Taras, 1989).

A classwide reward system may allow students to earn a "point" (e.g., sticker, smiley face, check mark, ticket) for displaying the targeted positive behavior, for not engaging in a particular negative behavior, or for performing a certain task/skill. Each student may be required to accumulate a specified number of points in order to obtain a reward (e.g., extra computer time, choice time, access to a preferred item). To further enhance motivation, a reward menu may remind students of the various rewards that they can earn. See Figure 2.46 for more examples. The specific details (e.g., the format that will be used, the number of points needed to obtain the reward, the reinforcers that will be provided) of the point system are typically determined by the teacher, according to the needs of individual students and the group.

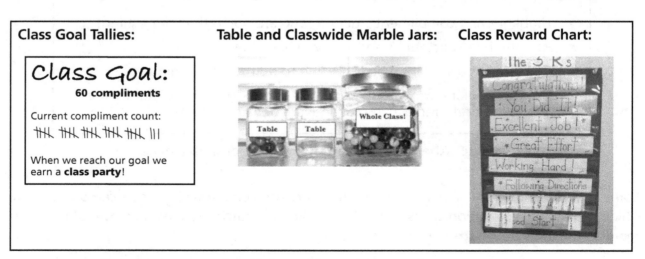

Figure 2.46. Examples of classwide positive reinforcement systems.

When using these systems, especially early on, it is important to provide the child with frequent opportunities to experience success. This will make the system more motivating for the student, thereby increasing the likelihood that he will actively participate in the reinforcement system. Punitive systems (i.e., those in which "points" or rewards are removed or opportunities to earn rewards are restricted) should not be used.

A common punitive system that should not be used is the "traffic light" procedure, where students' names are put on a traffic light and students are moved down from green (good behavior) to yellow (warning) to red (consequence). These punitive-based systems focus on the negative, rather than celebrating positive behavior. In addition, they do not teach the child what they should be doing as an alternative to their undesired behavior or explain why what they are doing is not okay for the classroom.

Individual Reinforcement Systems

Some students need an additional layer of support. The use of behavior charts can serve as an effective way to provide them with a more individualized means of receiving positive reinforcement.

Behavior chart. A behavior chart (see following page) is a tool used to track, reward, and encourage specific desired behaviors. There are many considerations for creating and implementing this type of individualized reinforcement system, including:

- *Make it positive.* The point of the chart is to emphasize positive behaviors, not the negative ones.

- *Make it motivating and fun.* Ensure the rewards are highly reinforcing for the student (i.e., something worth earning!). For younger children, make it a game. With older students, involve them in designing the chart or system for self-monitoring.

- *Make it interesting.* Variety is the spice of life! Remember to change it up often so the system remains rewarding. Vary your reward options to keep it novel.

- *Make it easy and attainable.* Ensure success (especially early on) to enhance motivation.

- *Make it easily visible.* Hang the chart in a location that is readily visible. Teachers and staff need to remember to utilize the chart and to model consistency by keeping up with the chart.

- *Make it specific.* Be specific in stating your expectations and make sure that the student has a clear understanding of expectations and how the chart is used.

- *Make it clear and realistic.* Tell the student exactly how she can earn rewards; that is, what counts and what doesn't. Don't require perfection. Highlight achievement, even if the student achieves the goal only three out of five days.

- *Make expectations attainable.* Avoid including too many expectations or tasks that may overwhelm the student and reduce his/her motivation. We want the student to experience success early on.

My Goals	Mon	Tues	Wed	Thurs	Fri
Hang up my jacket	✔	✔			
Put my lunchbox in the lunch bin	✔	✔			
Unpack my bookbag	✔	✔			
Put my folders in the color-coded bins	✔	✔			
Complete the "Do Now"	✔	✔			

Danny's Train Tickets — Unpacking Routine

Figure 2.47. Behavior chart.

Remember:

- *Keep it simple.* For younger students, the reward chart and recognition may be reinforcing enough to start.

- *Be creative.* Incorporate students' interests, thereby increasing their motivation to participate in the system.

- *Be consistent.* Once you start a chart, follow through. If the chart is a weekly chart, finish through the week. It will only be effective if it is used consistently!

- *Focus on rewards.* Focus on EARNING rather than losing or taking things away.

- *Remember that change takes time.* Set up a point or reward system that is fair and realistic for both your student and for you! If you cannot consistently implement the strategy (i.e., reward system), it is not realistic nor practical for your classroom. Find another method that works better for everyone involved. For example, if you and your co-teacher are not remembering to put stickers on your students' sticker charts when the charts are posted on the back bulletin board, consider another place for the charts (maybe on the student's desks) or for the stickers (on the students' hands or on their homework folders). The students and the systems need you to be consistent, so it is important to find a way to make it work for everyone.

Using the Classroom Guideposts

In the ASD Nest model, the Classroom Guideposts are first encountered by new staff in a course on ASD given during the summer before they begin working in the program. Staff who are hired too late to take the summer course are introduced to the Guideposts during a 2.5-day training workshop just before the beginning of the school year.

The Classroom Guideposts are identified to new staff as the additional curriculum for students with ASD that is infused throughout each school day. During both the course and the training workshop, new staff work in small groups to read and discuss sections of the Guideposts document (which is given to all trainees), addressing such questions as:

- Which strategies are familiar to you, and how have you used them or seen them being used?

- Which strategies are new to you, and do you now understand the why, when, and how to use them?

- What strategies that you have used or seen in use before would you use differently? In what way would you use them differently and why?

- What questions do you have about using the Guideposts?

The whole group then reconvenes to discuss the major themes and questions about implementing the Guideposts that arose in the small groups. The course instructor or workshop facilitator then provides training on the strategies outlined in the Guideposts along with how these strategies are implemented in accordance to the ASD Nest Three-Tier System, which is discussed in Chapter Three.

Aside from its use in training new program staff, the Classroom Guideposts document serves as a resource/reference in team meetings at which case conferences on individual students take place, as well as in the coaching of teachers by ASD Nest consultants.

For other useful planning guides to serving students with ASD, see the CAPS System (Henry & Myles, 2013) and the Ziggurat Model (Aspy & Grossman, 2011).

Conclusion

The ASD Nest Classroom Guideposts serve multiple functions. First and foremost, they are a tool for helping children with ASD. They are also a tool for supporting teachers and teams as they strive to achieve optimal outcomes for their students. Further, the Classroom Guideposts document serves as an orientation and training tool for new staff. It communicates to them what this intervention program is all about: its organizing philosophy about children with ASD and how to intervene to help them – an important aspect of any intervention model, but one that too many programs lack. Finally, the Guideposts document serves as a resource for ongoing professional development of the ASD Nest teams, as they use it to select and implement strategies and supports to match individual and group needs.

We would like to thank the following teachers for giving us permission to use photographs of their classrooms for this chapter: S. Boylan, J. Cecere, E. Clemente, A. Lanou, A. Lopez, A. Mittenthal, T. Murray, M. Paterno, J. Pollock, K. Ramirez, S. Tobin, D. Wattenberg, R. Youssef.

Chapter 3

Three-Tier Model of Supports for the ASD Nest Program

Lauren Hough, Jamie Bleiweiss, and Shirley Cohen

The Three-Tier Model of Supports for the ASD Nest Program was introduced in Chapter 1. As described, this is the ASD Nest Program's adaptation of response to intervention (RTI) (Fuchs & Fuchs, 2006) within the framework of positive behavior support (Carr et al., 2002). The model provides guidelines for which strategies and supports from the ASD Nest Classroom Guideposts to use with a class and which to use with individual students, along with when and why.

In this chapter, we describe the Three-Tier Model in more detail, present the forms used in implementing it, and explain how each part of the model is used. The components of the Three-Tier Model are as follows:

- Tier I Classroom Checklist of Strategies and Supports for ASD Nest Classes

- Tier I Checklist of Strategies and Supports for Individual Student Planning

- Tier II Checklist of Strategies and Supports for Individual Student Planning

- Tier III Checklist of Strategies and Supports for Individual Student Planning

The strategies in the checklists are organized into four support categories: social, behavioral, academic, and sensory functioning/self-regulation. Embedded in the use of the Three-Tier Model are two additional tools: An Academic Screening Form and a Functional Behavior Assessment Interview, both used when Tier III intervention is being considered.

Let's begin by looking at the Tier I Classroom Checklist of Strategies and Supports.

Using the Tier I Classroom Checklist of Strategies and Supports

The primary function of the Tier I Classroom Checklist of Strategies and Supports for ASD Classes is to help ensure fidelity of implementation of the ASD Nest Model. In addition, it is used in the professional development of staff.

The Tier I Classroom Checklist assesses whether relevant strategies and supports from the Classroom Guideposts are being implemented fully and appropriately. While the Classroom Guideposts were created particularly with children on the autism spectrum in mind, they encompass strategies and supports that are useful with all students in ASD Nest classes.

The Tier I Classroom Checklist was designed to be used by an ASD Nest Program consultant during an observation period of about 50 minutes. The consultant focuses on Level A strategies, which should always be readily observable in any given period. He/she may also note the use of Level B strategies, which are supplemental supports that may be relevant to a particular classroom.

After finishing the observation and completing the Tier I Classroom Checklist, the consultant meets with the teachers to highlight the Guidepost supports used well and to discuss the strategies not observed or used only occasionally, and thus representing missed opportunities for implementation. If the number of Level A strategies needing attention is large, the focus will primarily be on strengthening Level A strategies. If the number of Level A strategies that need strengthening is minimal, the discussion also includes Level B strategies that reflect missed opportunities. The consultant follows up on the discussion and the recommendations emanating from it through another classroom observation visit a few weeks later.

For programs that do not have ASD consultants, the observer completing the Tier I Classroom Checklist may be an experienced and highly respected member of the school's ASD team who is selected by that team, and the teachers who are observed may decide to have the discussion following the observation take place at an ASD team meeting so that all team members can benefit from it.

Still another way of using the Tier I Classroom Checklist is for self-monitoring – the teachers complete the Classroom Checklist themselves and then review the strategies they are using well and those that they are not using or not using well enough. After doing that, the teachers formulate a plan for making better use of strategies in situations that represent missed opportunities. They may also choose to share their self-study and the plan developed from it with the whole team.

Tier I

**Tier I
Classroom Checklist
ASD Nest Program
Three-Tier Model**

Tier I Strategies and Supports for ASD Nest Classes
The Tier I Classroom Checklist is used by the ASD Nest consultant to ensure full implementation of the Tier I strategies of the ASD Nest Three-Tier Model. The ASD Nest consultant uses this tool to ensure that the strategies are being used consistently to support students. There is no expectation that every strategy will be implemented during all lessons and activities in every classroom but rather that the strategies will be used frequently, whenever relevant, before more intensive individualized supports are pursued.

The Tier I strategies and supports in this checklist are divided into two levels, A & B, in each of the four domains (Sensory, Behavior, Social, Academic):
    Level A supports should <u>always</u> be present and readily observable during a 45- to 50-minute classroom visit.
    Level B supports are <u>additional</u> strategies that <u>may</u> be implemented in the classroom.

Directions for Using the Tier I Classroom Checklist:
1. Fill out class information requested at the top of the form on the next page.
2. Complete the checklist across all four domains as follows: For each item, indicate whether the strategy was **Observed** or **Not observed** by checking the appropriate box.
    ☐   **Observed** (for applicable items, indicate if it was used **"consistently"** or **"on occasion"**)
    ☐   **Not observed** (for applicable items, indicate **"missed opportunity"** and specify further in the Notes column)
3. Circle all Level A strategies that were either **Not observed** or were observed **"on occasion"** to identify the items that need further attention.
4. Meet with the teachers to highlight effective supports being used and to review a manageable number of Level A strategies and supports not yet implemented or implemented inconsistently. The ASD school team works with the teachers and the consultant to plan for more consistent use of the targeted Tier I strategies.
5. Follow up on implementation of suggested strategies and supports at the next classroom visit.

*Expanded definitions for underlined terms in the Tier I Classroom Checklist may be found in Chapter 2.

Figure 3.1. **Tier I Strategies and Supports for ASD Nest Classes.**

Tier I	Classroom: _____ Subject(s)/Activities: _____
	Completed by: _____ Date & Time: _____

Sensory Functioning & Self-Regulation Supports		Notes
LEVEL A: Supports that should *always* be present and observable in each 45- to 50-minute observation period:		
1. Classroom environment accommodates sensory sensitivities and prevents sensory overload.	☐ Observed ☐ Not observed	
2. Arousing and calming activities are balanced across the period.	☐ Observed ☐ Not observed	
3. <u>Break area</u> is inviting, available for student use, and offers materials for calming.	☐ Observed ☐ Not observed	

4. Teachers modify voice volume appropriate to individual students and to the size of the group.	☐ Observed
	  ☐ Consistently
	  ☐ On occasion
	☐ Not observed	

5. Opportunities are created for whole-class movement (e.g., movement break or transition between rug/desk).	☐ Observed ☐ Not observed: ☐ Missed opportunity	
LEVEL B: *Additional* support strategies that *may* be implemented:		
6. Relaxation activities are used to develop strategies for self-regulation.	☐ Observed ☐ Not observed: ☐ Missed opportunity	
7. Sensory tools are used by/available to students (e.g., work carrels, headphones, fidgets).	☐ Observed ☐ Not observed: ☐ Missed opportunity	

Figure 3.1. Tier I Strategies and Supports for ASD Nest Classes *(cont.).*

Behavioral Supports		Notes
LEVEL A: Supports that should *always* be present and observable in each 50-minute observation period:		
1. Classroom is organized to minimize visual distraction.	☐ Observed ☐ Not observed	

2. Daily <u>class schedule</u> is displayed and referenced as a transition/refocusing support.	☐ Observed
	  ☐ Consistently
	  ☐ On occasion
	☐ Not observed	

3. <u>Visual aids</u> and concrete examples are utilized to supplement verbal directions.	☐ Observed
	  ☐ Consistently
	  ☐ On occasion
	☐ Not observed	

4. Students are told what *to do* rather than what *not to do.*	☐ Observed
	  ☐ Consistently
	  ☐ On occasion
	☐ Not observed	

5. Clear, concise, concrete language is used to clarify expectations.	☐ Observed
	  ☐ Consistently
	  ☐ On occasion
	☐ Not observed	

6. Teachers "<u>catch students being good</u>," providing behavior-specific praise.	☐ Observed
	  ☐ Consistently
	  ☐ On occasion
	☐ Not observed	

7. Appropriate behavior in peers is highlighted.	☐ Observed
	  ☐ Consistently
	  ☐ On occasion
	☐ Not observed	

8. <u>Classwide reinforcement system</u> with clear, concrete behavioral expectations is used.	☐ Observed
	  ☐ Consistently
	  ☐ On occasion
	☐ Not observed	

9. Upcoming activities/transitions/expectations are previewed.	☐ Observed ☐ Not observed	
10. <u>5-Point Scales</u> are created and referenced to concretize abstract concepts (e.g., voice volume, level of control, size of a problem).	☐ Observed ☐ Not observed: ☐ Missed opportunity	
11. Opportunities are provided for students to make choices.	☐ Observed ☐ Not observed	

Figure 3.1. **Tier I Strategies and Supports for ASD Nest Classes** *(cont.).*

Behavioral Supports		Notes
LEVEL B: *Additional* support strategies that *may* be implemented:		
12. Visual task sequencing boards are used for routines and activities.	☐ Observed ☐ Not observed: ☐ Missed opportunity	
13. Nurturing peer buddies are used to provide support.	☐ Observed ☐ Not observed: ☐ Missed opportunity	

14. Student strengths and interests are incorporated into learning activities.	☐ Observed
	   ☐ Consistently
	   ☐ On occasion
	☐ Not observed
	   ☐ Missed opportunity	

15. Proximity control/signal interference is used as a prevention strategy.	☐ Observed ☐ Not observed ☐ Missed opportunity	
16. "Looking forward to" approach is used to help students anticipate upcoming, preferred activities.	☐ Observed ☐ Not observed ☐ Missed opportunity	
17. Visual timers are used for classroom transitions and activities to clearly display length/passage of time.	☐ Observed ☐ Not observed ☐ Missed opportunity	

Figure 3.1. Tier I Strategies and Supports for ASD Nest Classes *(cont.).*

Social Supports		Notes
LEVEL A: Supports that should *always* be present and observable in each 50-minute observation period:		

1. <u>Nonverbal language</u> is used (e.g., eye gaze, gestures, facial expressions).	☐ Observed
	   ☐ Consistently
	   ☐ On occasion
	☐ Not observed	

2. Strategies and supports that foster a classroom community/team are used (e.g., "we" language, table names, room themes, photos of shared experiences).	☐ Observed
	   ☐ Consistently
	   ☐ On occasion
	☐ Not observed	

3. Indirect prompts (e.g., declarative statements or gestures) are used.	☐ Observed
	   ☐ Consistently
	   ☐ On occasion
	☐ Not observed	

4. Students are given extra time to process and respond to language in social situations (e.g., transitioning, talking to a peer/teacher at desks).	☐ Observed
	   ☐ Consistently
	   ☐ On occasion
	☐ Not observed	

5. <u>Experience-sharing</u> language is used (e.g., <u>celebrating</u>, <u>labeling the moment</u>, teamwork).	☐ Observed ☐ Not observed	
6. Teachers foster social engagement (e.g., building anticipation and excitement, remembering shared experiences).	☐ Observed ☐ Not observed	
LEVEL B: *Additional* support strategies that *may* be implemented:		
7. <u>Declarative language</u> is used to invite experience-sharing.	☐ Observed ☐ Not observed ☐ Missed opportunity	
8. <u>Self-talk</u> is used to model Social Thinking® (Winner, 2005) and problem-solving.	☐ Observed ☐ Not observed ☐ Missed opportunity	
9. Basic Social Thinking® (Winner, 2005) language, *appropriate* for the grade, is used (e.g., <u>flexibility</u>, <u>thinking about me/you</u>® (Winner, 2007), <u>listening with your whole body</u>).	☐ Observed ☐ Not observed ☐ Missed opportunity	
10. Small-group teamwork/problem-solving experiences are facilitated, providing adult support, using developmentally appropriate Social Thinking® (Winner, 2005) language and strategies.	☐ Observed ☐ Not observed ☐ Missed opportunity	
11. Role-play is used with the whole class/small groups to prepare for a new/difficult situation (e.g., fire drill, working with a partner, playing a math game).	☐ Observed ☐ Not observed ☐ Missed opportunity	
12. <u>Social narratives</u> and <u>cartooning</u> are used.	☐ Observed ☐ Not observed ☐ Missed opportunity	

Figure 3.1. **Tier I Strategies and Supports for ASD Nest Classes** *(cont.).*

Academic/Curriculum Supports		Notes
LEVEL A: Supports that should *always* be present and observable in each 50-minute observation period:		
1. Teachers use variety of <u>co-teaching styles</u> (e.g., one teach-one assist, parallel teaching).	☐ Observed ☐ Not observed	
2. Mini-lessons are structured to promote active engagement, to assess mastery, and to help teachers differentiate their instruction. Mini-lessons contain: (a) clear teaching point, (b) modeling, (c) guided student practice, (d) independent student practice, and (e) student share.	☐ Observed ☐ Not observed	

3. Lessons are well planned, and all materials related to the lesson and student work are ready and easily accessible.	☐ Observed
	  ☐ Consistently
	  ☐ On occasion
	☐ Not observed	

4. General visuals are used to clarify expectations and academic concepts during lessons and individual/group work times.	☐ Observed
	  ☐ Consistently
	  ☐ On occasion
	☐ Not observed	

5. Extra time is provided to students for processing and responding to oral communication.	☐ Observed
	  ☐ Consistently
	  ☐ On occasion
	☐ Not observed	

6. Directions for independent work are clear and concise. The number of steps in directions is limited, considering student age as well as language processing and cognitive levels.	☐ Observed
	  ☐ Consistently
	  ☐ On occasion
	☐ Not observed	

7. Pace of the lesson is appropriate for the students in the class.	☐ Observed ☐ Not observed	
8. The amount of independent work is appropriate for the students' grade and level of academic readiness.	☐ Observed ☐ Not observed	
9. Seating is planned strategically to facilitate <u>peer support</u>.	☐ Observed ☐ Not observed	
10. Expectations for what students should do when they are finished with independent work are clear.	☐ Observed ☐ Not observed	

Figure 3.1. **Tier I Strategies and Supports for ASD Nest Classes** *(cont.).*

Academic/Curriculum Supports		Notes
LEVEL B: *Additional* support strategies that *may* be implemented:		
11. Complex academic activities are broken down (<u>task analysis</u>) to clarify and enumerate component steps and sequences.	☐ Observed ☐ Not observed ☐ Missed opportunity	
12. Manipulatives are used to clarify concepts and increase active engagement.	☐ Observed ☐ Not observed ☐ Missed opportunity	
13. Presentation of academic activities/tasks is modified to incorporate students' interests, strengths, or learning styles.	☐ Observed ☐ Not observed ☐ Missed opportunity	
14. Supports for asking for help are used.	☐ Observed ☐ Not observed ☐ Missed opportunity	
15. Graphic organizers are used for organizing, planning, and reflecting.	☐ Observed ☐ Not observed ☐ Missed opportunity	
16. Flexible small groups are used for differentiating instruction.	☐ Observed ☐ Not observed ☐ Missed opportunity	
17. New, challenging material and/or content is previewed prior to instruction.	☐ Observed ☐ Not observed ☐ Missed opportunity	
18. Students are given the opportunity to work in small groups with the necessary supports.	☐ Observed ☐ Not observed ☐ Missed opportunity	
19. Whole-class response strategies are used in lessons (e.g., slates).	☐ Observed ☐ Not observed ☐ Missed opportunity	
20. Timers are used for independent work time cuing (by teachers).	☐ Observed ☐ Not observed ☐ Missed opportunity	

Figure 3.1. **Tier I Strategies and Supports for ASD Nest Classes** *(cont.).*

Using the Tier I Checklist of Strategies and Supports for Individual Students

The primary function of the Tier I Checklist of Strategies and Supports for Individual Student Planning is to help teachers and other staff of ASD Nest Programs make smart decisions about how to best intervene with particular students in their areas of greatest need. This checklist was designed to focus on students who are not moving at an adequate pace toward meeting IEP goals and class/grade expectations, or who are engaging in behavior that significantly interferes with their own learning and/or that of their classmates.

The checklist for individual students includes the same strategies as the Tier I Classroom Checklist but elicits different types of responses from staff. For example, it asks for identification of strategies and supports that are of special relevance for a particular child, along with recommendations for strengthening them and/or adding others, to try to achieve a better outcome. This is a team task. Figure 3.2 presents the Tier I Checklist for Individual Student Planning.

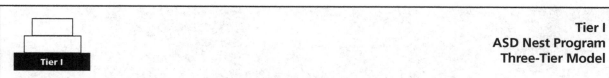

Tier I
ASD Nest Program
Three-Tier Model

Tier I

Tier I Checklist for Individual Student Planning: *Relevant for All Nest Classes*

This individual student form is to be completed by the student's teachers and other members of the school team for planning more effective use of Tier I strategies. Team members identify the strategies across all four domains that are most relevant to help support the student. For each of those strategies, indicate whether it should be continued, modified, or added to the student's intervention plan by placing a checkmark in the appropriate column, in accordance with the key below. Comments on implementation recommendations may be added in the column on the right, entitled "Notes on Implementation."

Recommendations		
C	**M**	**A**
Continue *current use of support*	**Modify** *existing support (Increase or decrease)*	**Add** *as a new support*

Student Name: _____ **Date:** _____

Sensory Functioning & Self-Regulation Supports	Identify Strategies That Are Most Relevant			Notes on Implementation
	C	**M**	**A**	
1. Modify classroom environments to accommodate sensory sensitivities and prevent sensory overload.				
2. Balance arousing and calming activities across the day.				
3. Create and promote the use of a <u>break area</u> that contains calming materials for self-regulation.				
4. Monitor teacher voice volume so that it is appropriate to individuals in the class and to the size of the group.				
5. Utilize whole-class movement activities throughout the day.				
6. Use classroom relaxation activities throughout the day.				
7. Make <u>sensory tools</u> available, as appropriate (e.g., work carrels, headphones, fidgets).				

Figure 3.2. **Tier I Checklist for Individual Student Planning.**

Behavioral Supports	Identify Strategies That Are Most Relevant			Notes on Implementation
	C	M	A	
1. Display daily class schedule and reference frequently.				
2. Organize classroom to minimize visual distraction.				
3. Utilize visual aids and concrete examples to supplement verbal directions.				
4. Provide opportunities for students to make choices throughout the day.				
5. Incorporate student strengths & interests into learning activities.				
6. Tell students what *to do* rather than what *not to do.*				
7. Use clear, concise, concrete language to clarify expectations.				
8. "Catch them being good" and provide behavior-specific praise.				
9. Use proximity control/signal interference preventively.				
10. Highlight appropriate behavior in peers.				
11. Anticipate upcoming preferred activities ("looking forward to" approach).				
12. Preview upcoming activities/transitions/expectations.				
13. Use and refer to the Incredible 5-Point Scale to concretize abstract concepts.				
14. Use visual task sequencing boards for routines and activities.				
15. Select nurturing peer buddies to provide support.				
16. Use classwide visual timers for transitions and activities to indicate activity duration.				
17. Implement classwide reinforcement system (e.g., reward chart) that has clear, concrete expectations, spelling out specific behaviors/skills to be reinforced.				

Figure 3.2. **Tier I Checklist for Individual Student Planning** *(cont.).*

Social Supports	Identify Strategies That Are Most Relevant			Notes on Implementation
	C	M	A	
1. Use <u>nonverbal language</u> and communication to promote referencing and engagement.				
2. Use strategies and supports that foster a classroom community/team (e.g., "we" language, table names, room themes, photos of shared experiences).				
3. Foster <u>social engagement</u> (e.g., building anticipation, encoding and revisiting shared memories).				
4. Provide students with extra time to process and respond to language in social situations.				
5. Use experience-sharing language (e.g., <u>celebrating</u>, <u>labeling the moment</u>, teamwork).				
6. Use <u>declarative language</u> to foster experience-sharing.				
7. Use <u>self-talk</u> to model Social Thinking® (Winner, 2005), language, and problem-solving.				
8. Use indirect prompts such as declarative statements, gestures, eye gaze, and physical proximity to enhance social awareness.				
9. Use basic Social Thinking® (Winner, 2005) language *appropriate* for the grade (e.g., <u>flexibility</u>, <u>thinking about me/you</u>® (Winner, 2007), <u>listening with your whole body</u>).				
10. Facilitate teamwork and problem-solving experiences in small groups using developmentally appropriate Social Thinking® (Winner, 2005) language and strategies.				
11. Lead whole class/small groups in <u>role-playing</u> new/difficult situations.				
12. <u>Social narratives</u> and/or <u>cartooning</u> are used to support some students to highlight the social aspects of a situation.				

Figure 3.2.* Tier I Checklist for Individual Student Planning *(cont.).

Academic/Curriculum Supports	Identify Strategies That Are Most Relevant			Notes on Implementation
	C	M	A	
1. Utilize a *variety* of <u>co-teaching styles</u> (e.g., one teach-one assist; parallel group).				
2. Collaboratively plan lessons and prepare all necessary materials to ensure that everything is ready and easily accessible.				
3. Use mini-lesson structure for academic lesson, providing a clear teaching point, modeling, facilitating guided practice, allowing for independent student practice, and then reconvening for a share after independent/group work.				
4. Preview new, challenging material and/or content prior to instruction.				
5. Use flexible small groups to differentiate instruction.				
6. Plan seating strategically to facilitate peer support.				
7. Allow extra time for processing and responding to oral communication.				
8. Provide clear, concise directions for independent work, limiting the number of steps in directions and considering student age, cognitive, and language processing levels.				
9. Use a variety of visuals to clarify lesson, individual, and group work expectations/academic concepts.				
10. Modify presentation of academic activities/tasks to incorporate interests, strengths, or learning styles.				
11. Use graphic organizers for organizing, planning, and reflecting.				
12. Use manipulatives across lessons, whenever relevant, to clarify concepts and increase active engagement.				
13. Use whole-class response strategies in lessons (e.g., slates).				
14. <u>Task analyze</u> complex academic activities to clarify component steps and sequences.				
15. Provide supports to facilitate students' asking for help.				
16. Utilize timers for independent work time cuing.				
17. Pace lessons and amount of independent work required so that it is appropriate for the students' grade and level of academic readiness.				
18. Provide clear expectations for what students should do when they are finished with their independent work.				
19. Provide opportunities for students to work in small groups with the necessary supports.				

Figure 3.2. **Tier I Checklist for Individual Student Planning** *(cont.).*

While planning is essential, it is sometimes not enough, so follow-up is needed. About three to four weeks after the recommended supports for a student have been put into operation, the team reconvenes to assess whether the supports have proven sufficient to achieve better outcomes for the target child. A Check-In Form is completed at that meeting, with a recommendation for next steps. If the child is making the progress sought, his Tier I individual intervention plan is continued. If the child has not achieved the progress sought, Tier II strategies are added to the plan for that student. Figure 3.3 presents the Tier I Implementation Check-In Form.

Tier I Implementation Check-In Form

The first Tier I implementation check-in should take place approximately 3-4 weeks after the student's plan has been implemented. After that, if the student continues to make progress, check-in meetings can take place every 5-6 weeks.

Student: _____ **Date:** _____

Have the recommended strategies and supports (additions/modifications) been implemented?

How did the student respond to the interventions? Have any improvements in the previously identified areas of concern taken place? If so, describe those changes by giving specific examples.

Next step in supporting this student: Provide the team's recommendation(s).

Figure 3.3. Tier I Implementation Check-In Form.

Using The Tier II Checklist of Strategies and Supports for Individual Students

Tier II strategies and supports were designed for students who make only limited progress in meeting goals and expectations after implementation of their individual Tier I plans. The Tier I Implementation Check-In Form completed at a follow-up meeting to look at the student's progress will contain a recommendation for either continuing to serve a student through his Tier I individual plan or for the addition of Tier II supports. The recommendation for Tier II supports is made after it has been determined that the student's Tier I individual plan has been adequately implemented but has not been sufficient to advance progress toward meeting IEP goals and class/grade expectations.

Several additional strategies are introduced in Tier II, along with increases in the intensity of implementation of selected Tier I strategies. One example of an additional strategy is a sensory story. (See item #4 in the section on Sensory Functioning and Self-Regulation Supports in Figure 3.4.) A sensory story is a narrative that describes a challenging sensory experience for an individual child and offers possible strategies for coping with it.

Tier II supports are often implemented in groups of two or three students and sometimes require one-to-one instruction initially. A positive stance and encouraging communication must pervade the delivery of Tier II strategies if they are to be effective. Figure 3.4 presents the Tier II Checklist for Individual Student Planning.

**Tier II
ASD Nest Program
Three-Tier Model**

Tier II Strategies and Supports: Individualized, Planned Interventions

The following Tier II strategies are used with individual students who require additional, planned interventions and supports. Movement from Tier I to Tier II supports in any domain requires (a) completion of the Tier I Checklist; (b) review and discussion of Tier I Checklist at a team meeting; and (c) determination that Tier I supports across domains have been implemented adequately and found insufficient to meet the student's needs. Communication with a parent or guardian is also recommended.

Team members should identify the strategies across all four domains that are most relevant to help support the student. For each of those strategies, indicate whether it should be continued, modified, or added to the student's intervention plan by placing a checkmark in the appropriate column, in accordance with the key below. Comments on implementation recommendations may be added in the column on the right, entitled "Notes on Implementation."

Recommendations		
C	**M**	**A**
Continue current use of support	*Modify* existing support (Increase or decrease)	*Add* as a new support

Student Name: _____ **Date**:_____

Sensory Functioning & Self-Regulation Supports	Identify Strategies That Are Most Relevant			Notes on Implementation
	C	M	A	
1. Implement individual <u>sensory diet/relaxation program</u> created by occupational therapist (OT) requiring teacher supervision and monitoring by OT therapist.				
2. Use individual <u>sensory tools</u> as directed by OT (e.g., bump seats, wedges, pencil grips, OT vests, slant boards).				
3. Create and use private work space, separate from peers.				
4. Utilize individualized <u>sensory stories</u>.				

Figure 3.4. Tier II Checklist for Individual Student Planning.

Behavioral Supports	Identify Strategies That Are Most Relevant			Notes on Implementation
	C	M	A	
1. Provide individualized <u>mini-schedules</u> with teacher support throughout the day.				
2. Use individualized <u>task boards</u> for activities/procedures with teacher monitoring.				
3. Use individualized visual aid reminders to clarify expectations.				
4. Provide individualized, planned priming for new/ challenging tasks.				
5. Modify and/or simplify challenging tasks.				
6. Provide individualized, planned opportunities for student choice.				
7. Use <u>timers</u> on an individualized basis for specific activities/tasks.				
8. Implement "<u>antiseptic bouncing</u>"/ "<u>just walk, don't talk</u>" strategies.				
9. Implement planned use of <u>high-probability requests</u> to precede challenging activities.				
10. Use individualized and comprehensive <u>planned peer-based supports.</u>				
11. Create and strategically use <u>Incredible 5-Point Scales</u> tailored to individual student needs.				
12. Provide functional communication training (e.g., the <u>HELP program</u> and <u>break program).</u>				
13. Use <u>individualized behavior reinforcement system.</u>				
14. Create and use individual <u>social narrative</u> books as a preventative measure (see also use of social narratives in Tier II social domain).				

Figure 3.4. Tier II Checklist for Individual Student Planning *(cont.).*

Social Supports	Identify Strategies That Are Most Relevant			Notes on Implementation
	C	M	A	
1. Use individualized visuals, <u>Power Cards</u>, problem-solving frameworks (e.g., <u>S.O.C.C.S.S.</u>, <u>social autopsies</u>), <u>cartooning</u>, **or** <u>Social Behavior Mapping</u>© (Winner, 2005) with individual students to clarify social situations and enhance coping skills.				
2. Create <u>social narrative</u> books written for and in collaboration with individual students (books can be made up of compiled social narratives written for a particular child) for continued use and reference.				
3. Use 1:1 or small group <u>role play</u>, <u>video modeling</u>, reflection, and/or priming for new/difficult situations.				

Academic/Curriculum Supports	Identify Strategies That Are Most Relevant			Notes on Implementation
	C	M	A	
1. Provide one-to-one and small-group previewing for new/challenging content.				
2. Provide small-group instruction on a consistent basis for challenging content.				
3. Incorporate individual student interests to increase motivation.				
4. Use individualized visuals for lesson expectations and independent or group work expectations.				
5. Utilize individualized graphic organizers, simplified as needed.				
6. Provide differentiated and simplified content, as needed.				
7. Modify work expectations for product and, when needed (e.g., decreased amount of work required).				

Figure 3.4. **Tier II Checklist for Individual Student Planning** *(cont.).*

Academic/Curriculum Supports	Identify Strategies That Are Most Relevant			Notes on Implementation
	C	M	A	
8. Decrease expectation for time-on-task and/or duration of learning activities.				
9. Provide individualized note-taking supports for lessons.				
10. Provide teacher support during transitions by checking in with student to ensure understanding of next steps.				
11. Create checklists for student with complex tasks broken into steps/parts.				
12. Provide and monitor independent use of individual organizational systems by student (e.g., binders, color coded systems, bins).				
13. Establish a self-monitoring system to enhance active participation.				
14. Use timers for individual students to improve time management during work periods.				
15. Plan and implement specific peer supports.				

Figure 3.4. **Tier II Checklist for Individual Student Planning** *(cont.).*

When a student is receiving Tier II supports in the area of behavior, an SABC Chart is used to collect and record data about that student's functioning. SABC Charts are designed to gather day-to-day data that may help the team identify the sources of interfering behavior. The "S" in the form's title stands for *setting events* that make interfering behavior more likely to occur; the "A" stands for *antecedents*, events that immediately precede and may be triggers of interfering behavior; the "B" stands for behavior. Finally, the "C" stands for *consequences*, which are responses to the student's interfering behavior.

An analysis of data collected over a few days on SABC Charts may identify combinations of setting events, antecedents, and consequences that make it more likely that the child continues to engage in interfering behavior. An SABC Chart is shown in Figure 3.5.

Setting Events-Antecedent-Behavior-Consequence (SABC)

Please fill out the following data chart as soon as possible following any disruptive or interfering behavior. The information you provide for each section of the table will help us create a comprehensive picture of the circumstances triggering and maintaining the targeted behavior.

Student's Name: _____ **Target Behavior:** _____

Context (Briefly describe the time, activity, nature and place of the activity or task)		Setting Events (Describe **biological, environmental, social factors** that may contribute to the behavior)	Antecedent (What **immediately** precedes the event?)	Target Behavior (Measurable observable terms; **frequency, duration, intensity**)	Consequence (**Response/reaction** to the behavior; what happened afterwards?)
Time:	**Activity/ Task:**				
Time:	**Activity/ Task:**				
Time:	**Activity/ Task:**				

Figure 3.5. Setting Events-Antecedent-Behavior-Consequence Chart (SABC).

The data collected through the SABC Chart are used at a follow-up meeting about the student about three weeks after Tier II supports were instituted. Based on the data, as well as reports from teachers and other team members who work with the student, a decision is made on whether to add Tier III supports in the area of behavior. That recommendation is subsequently recorded on the Tier II Implementation Check-In Form. Figure 3.6 presents the Tier II Implementation Check-In Form.

Tier II Implementation Check-In Form

The first Tier II implementation check-in should take place approximately 3-4 weeks after the student's plan has been implemented. After that, if the student continues to make progress, check-in meetings can take place every 5-6 weeks.

Student: _____ **Date:** _____

Have the recommended strategies and supports (additions/modifications) been implemented?

How did the student respond to the interventions? Have any improvements in the previously identified areas of concern taken place? If so, describe those changes by giving specific examples.

Next step in supporting this student: Provide the team's recommendation(s).

Figure 3.6. Tier II Implementation Check-In Form.

Using the Tier III Checklist of Strategies and Supports for Individual Students

For a small number of children in ASD Nest Programs, Tier II strategies are also insufficient to support adequate progress in one, two, three, or even all four major areas. A student who is functioning well in any of those major areas can continue with the Tier II intervention plan for those areas while also receiving the much more intensive, individual supports of Tier III in the remaining area or areas.

Tier III interventions go beyond those in Tier II in intensity and frequency of use, although some new strategies may also be introduced; for example, a sensory schedule. A sensory schedule is a visual schedule for an individual child that lists a series of special activities implemented at frequent points over the course of the day. (See item #2 in the section on Sensory Functioning and Self-Regulation Supports in Figure 3.9). They are usually created in collaboration with an ASD consultant, and they generally include one-to-one teaching, monitoring, and reinforcement.

When the ASD team concludes that a student needs Tier III supports, a meeting is set up with the parent(s)/guardian to gather and share information. If the area of concern is academics, the parent(s) or guardian responds to the questions on the Tier III Academic Screening Form to the best of his/her ability at that meeting. This form is presented in Figure 3.7.

Tier III Academic Screening Form

Entry into any Tier III intervention *must* involve a parent/guardian meeting to gather and share information about supports and strategies to be used. The team must also meet to complete this form for the student's file prior to implementing any Tier III strategies. All Tier III interventions are intensive, individual supports for students who continue to struggle with most grade-level expectations and receive a rating of "1" (the lowest rating on a four-point scale) in reading, writing, or math on their report card. Supplemental programs for decoding, math, or writing may need to be considered to provide further support for the student.

Date: _____   Student Name: _____

Persons present at meeting: _____

Before considering Tier III Academic Interventions, the team must take the following into account and document actions taken to examine these possible contributing factors

POSSIBLE CONTRIBUTING FACTOR	If yes, person/s responsible & implementation	Initial when completed
Has there been a sudden change in the child's academic performance over the past several months? ❑ Yes ❑ No *Notes:*	Who: _____ What: _____ By when: _____	
Has the student's file (e.g., cumulative record) and/or recent assessments and observation reports been reviewed to identify possible sudden changes in the child's academic performance over the past several months? ❑ Yes ❑ No *Notes:*	Who: _____ What: _____ By when: _____	
Is there any indication that:		
A comprehensive medical and/or neurological evaluation might be needed? ❑ Yes ❑ No *Notes:*	Who: _____ What: _____ By when: _____	
A comprehensive vision evaluation might be needed (e.g., to rule out visual tracking difficulties, nearsightedness, farsightedness, convergence issues)? ❑ Yes ❑ No *Notes:*	Who: _____ What: _____ By when: _____	
An OT evaluation might be necessary? ❑ Yes ❑ No *Notes:*	Who: _____ What: _____ By when: _____	
An assistive technology evaluation might be needed? ❑ Yes ❑ No Notes:	Who: _____ What: _____ By when: _____	

Figure 3.7. Tier III Academic Screening Form.

If the child needs more intensive behavioral supports, the parent is asked to respond to questions on the Functional Behavioral Assessment Interview Form (Abridged Version). That form is presented in Figure 3.8.

Functional Behavior Assessment Interview Form (Abridged Version)
(Adapted from Dunlap et al., 2010; O'Neill et al., 1997)

Student's Name: _____   Date of Interview: _____

Person(s) Interviewed: _____   Interviewer: _____

Age: _____   Grade: _____

BACKGROUND INFORMATION

1. What are the student's strengths, skills, and interests (specify highly preferred events, items, people, activities)? _____
    _____
    _____

2. What are the student's challenges and areas of greatest difficulty? _____
    _____

3. What people, things, and activities does the student like most? _____
    _____
    _____

4. What people, things, and activities does the student like the least? _____
    _____
    _____

BEHAVIOR(S) OF CONCERN

1. Target behaviors interfering with learning and social functioning (in order of priority):

Target Behavior	Description (Operational definition)	Frequency (Circle one)	Duration (Minutes)	Intensity (Circle one)
		Multiple times a day Once a day Less than once a day	_____	High Medium Low
		Multiple times a day Once a day Less than once a day	_____	High Medium Low
		Multiple times a day Once a day Less than once a day	_____	High Medium Low

2. If multiple behaviors are listed, do these behaviors occur together in a predictable sequence? If so, briefly describe _____
    _____
    _____

3. **Precursor Behavior(s):** Identify any indicators (e.g., low-level disruptive behaviors, or a chain of behaviors) that reliably precede the target behavior. _____
    _____

Figure 3.8. Functional Behavior Assessment Interview Form (Bleiweiss & Tanol, 2012).

PREVENT COMPONENT: Part I – Identifying Setting Events

1a. Are there circumstances **unrelated to the school setting** that occur on some days and not other days that may make interfering behavior more likely?

☐ *Illness (specify)* ☐ *Allergies* ☐ *Missed dose of medication* ☐ *Change in medication*
☐ *Sleep difficulties* ☐ *Fatigue* ☐ *Hunger/thirst* ☐ *Restricted/specialized diet*
☐ *Biomedical supplements* ☐ *Diet change* ☐ *Hormonal changes/menses*
☐ *Sensory sensitivities (specify)*_____ ☐ *Change in routine*
☐ *Home conflict* ☐ *Parent not home* ☐ *Bus conflict*
☐ *Other (specify)*_____

1b. Provide a detailed description for any of the items you checked above. _____
_____
_____

2. Are there conditions in the **physical environment** that are associated with a high likelihood of interfering behavior? For example, too warm or too cold, too crowded, too much noise, too chaotic, weather condition
☐ *Yes (specify)* _____
☐ *No*

3a. Are there **times of the school day** when interfering behavior is **most likely** to occur? If yes, what are they?
☐ *Morning* ☐ *Before meals* ☐ *During meals* ☐ *After meals* ☐ *Arrival* ☐ *Afternoon*
☐ *Dismissal* ☐ *Other (specify):* _____

3b. Are there **times of the school day** when interfering behavior is **least likely** to occur? If yes, what are they?
☐ *Morning* ☐ *Before meals* ☐ *During meals* ☐ *After meals* ☐ *Arrival* ☐ *Afternoon*
☐ *Dismissal* ☐ *Other (specify):* _____

4a. Are there **specific activities** during which interfering behavior is **very likely** to occur? If yes, specify.
☐ *Reading/ELA* ☐ *Writing* ☐ *Math* ☐ *Science* ☐ *Independent work*
☐ *Small-group work* ☐ *Large-group work* ☐ *Riding the bus* ☐ *One-on-one* ☐ *Computer*
☐ *Recess* ☐ *Lunch* ☐ *Free time* ☐ *Peer/cooperative* ☐ *Centers*
☐ *Discussions/Q&A* ☐ *Worksheets* ☐ *Specials (specify)* _____
☐ *Transitions (specify)*_____ ☐ *Other:*_____

4b. Are there **specific activities** during which cooperative and prosocial behavior is **very likely** to occur? If yes, specify.
☐ *Reading/ELA* ☐ *Writing* ☐ *Math* ☐ *Science* ☐ *Independent work*
☐ *Small-group work* ☐ *Large-group work* ☐ *Riding the bus* ☐ *One-on-one* ☐ *Computer*
☐ *Recess* ☐ *Lunch* ☐ *Free time* ☐ *Peer/cooperative* ☐ *Centers*
☐ *Discussions/Q&A* ☐ *Worksheets* ☐ *Specials (specify)* _____
☐ *Transitions (specify)*_____ ☐ *Other:*_____

5a. Are there **specific classmates or adults** whose proximity is associated with a high likelihood of interfering behavior? If so, specify.
☐ *Peers (specify)*_____ ☐ *Teacher(s) (specify)* _____
☐ *OT*_____ ☐ *Speech therapist*_____
☐ *Bus or lunch aide*_____ ☐ *Other school staff (specify)*_____
☐ *Parent/guardian* ☐ *Sibling* ☐ *Other family member (specify)*_____
☐ *Other:*_____

5b. Are there **specific classmates or adults** whose proximity is associated with a high likelihood of cooperative and prosocial behavior? If so, who are they?
☐ *Peers (specify)*_____ ☐ *Teacher(s) (specify)* _____
☐ *OT*_____ ☐ *Speech therapist*_____
☐ *Bus or lunch aide*_____ ☐ *Other school staff (specify)*_____
☐ *Parent/guardian* ☐ *Sibling* ☐ *Other family member (specify)*_____
☐ *Other:*_____

Figure 3.8. Functional Behavior Assessment Interview Form *(cont.).*

PREVENT COMPONENT: Part II – Identifying Antecedents (triggers)

1. Are there **specific circumstances** that are associated with a high likelihood of interfering behavior (i.e., identify antecedents that are most likely to set off or trigger the behavior). Check all that apply.

   ☐ *Instructed to start task*　　☐ *Task too difficult*　　☐ *Novel task*
   ☐ *Task is repetitive (same daily)*　☐ *Being told work is wrong*　☐ *Task too long*
   ☐ *Task is boring*　　　　　☐ *Instructed to transition*　☐ *Reprimand or correction*
   ☐ *Told "no," "stop," "don't"*　☐ *Instructed to "wait"*　☐ *Unstructured time (down time)*
   ☐ *Seated near specific peer*　☐ *Peer teasing or comments*　☐ *Change in schedule*
   ☐ *Start of nonpreferred activity*　☐ *Denied access to preferred item*　☐ *Removal of preferred item*
   ☐ *End of preferred activity*　☐ *Unable to complete task*　☐ *Given unclear directions*
   ☐ *Communication not understood by others*
   ☐ *Sudden or unexpected sensory overstimulation (e.g., loud noise, bumped/touched by someone)*
   ☐ *Teacher is attending to others (reduced level of attention given)*
   ☐ *Presence or absence of certain person*_____
   ☐ *Other:* _____
   _____

TEACH COMPONENT: Part I – Identifying the Function of the Target Behavior

1. Does the interfering behavior seem to be exhibited in order to:
   - **Gain attention from peers or adults**?
     ☐ Yes *(list the specific peers and/or adults)* _____
     ☐ No
   - **Obtain access to certain objects or activities** (e.g., toys or games, materials, food)?
     ☐ Yes *(list specific objects)* _____
     ☐ No
   - **Delay (escape/avoid) a transition** from a preferred activity to a nonpreferred activity?
     ☐ Yes *(list specific transition)* _____
     ☐ No
   - **Terminate or delay (escape/avoid)** a non-preferred (e.g., difficult, boring, repetitive) task/activity?
     ☐ Yes *(list specific tasks/activities)* _____
     ☐ No
   - **Get away from (escape/avoid)** attention from a non-preferred classmate or adult?
     ☐ Yes *(list the specific peers or adults)* _____
     ☐ No

TEACH COMPONENT: Part II – Identifying Replacement Skills/Behavior

1. What **social skill(s)** could the student learn in order to reduce the likelihood of the interfering behavior occurring in the future?

   ☐ *Peer interaction*　　☐ *Sharing objects*　　☐ *Taking turns*
   ☐ *Play skills*　　　　☐ *Sharing attention*　☐ *Accepting differences*
   ☐ *Joint or shared attention*　☐ *Conversation skills*　☐ *Making prosocial statements*
   ☐ *Waiting for reinforcement*　☐ *Getting attention appropriately*　☐ *Losing gracefully*
   ☐ *Other:* _____
   _____

2. What **interfering-solving skill(s)** could the student learn in order to reduce the likelihood of the interfering behavior occurring in the future?

   ☐ *Recognizing need for help*　☐ *Note-taking strategies*　☐ *Staying engaged*
   ☐ *Asking for help*　　　☐ *Assignment management*　☐ *Working independently*
   ☐ *Ignoring peers*　　　☐ *Graphic organizers*　☐ *Working with a peer*
   ☐ *Making an outline*　　☐ *Self-management*　☐ *Using visual supports to work independently*
   ☐ *Move ahead to easier items, then go back to difficult items*
   ☐ *Making choices from several appropriate options*
   ☐ *Other:* _____

Figure 3.8. **Functional Behavior Assessment Interview Form** *(cont.).*

3. What **communication skill(s)** could the student learn in order to reduce the likelihood of the interfering behavior occurring in the future?

☐ Asking for a break ☐ Raising hand for attention ☐ Asking for help ☐ Requesting information
☐ Requesting wants ☐ Expressing likes & dislikes ☐ Active listening ☐ Commenting
☐ Responding to others ☐ Expressing emotions (frustration, anger, hurt)
☐ Other: _____
_____

REINFORCE COMPONENT: Part I – Identifying Consequences (responses)

1. What **consequence(s)** usually follow the student's interfering behavior (i.e., identify particular responses/ consequences that are most likely to follow the target behavior)? Check all that apply.
☐ Given teacher attention
   ☐ Redirected ☐ Reminded of rules/expectations ☐ Verbal reprimand/warning
   ☐ Correction ☐ Assistance given ☐ Calming/soothing comments provided
   ☐ Physical prompt
☐ Peer attention/reaction (e.g., laughing, negative reaction, reprimand, encouragement) Specify:_____
☐ Behavior ignored (i.e., attention withdrawn/removed)
☐ Given personal space (time to chill out/relax) ☐ Given access to an object/activity
☐ Request or directive delayed ☐ Request or directive (demand) withdrawn
☐ Delay in activity/task ☐ Activity/task changed ☐ Activity/task terminated
☐ Removed from activity or area ☐ Removed object or preferred item
☐ Removal of reinforcers ☐ Sent to office ☐ Sent home
☐ Natural consequences (specify) _____
☐ Other: _____

2. What is the likelihood of the student's **appropriate behavior** (e.g., on-task behavior, cooperation, successful performance) resulting in acknowledgment or praise from teachers or other school staff?
☐ Very likely ☐ Sometimes ☐ Seldom ☐ Never

3. What is the likelihood of the student's **interfering behavior** resulting in acknowledgment (e.g., reprimands, corrections) from teachers or other school staff?
☐ Very likely ☐ Sometimes ☐ Seldom ☐ Never

REINFORCE COMPONENT: Part II – Preference Assessment (Identifying reinforcers)

1. What school-related items and activities are **most enjoyable** to the student? What items or activities could serve as special rewards?
☐ Receives praise from adult ☐ Receives praise from peer ☐ Social interaction with adults
☐ Music ☐ Art activity ☐ Puzzles ☐ Computer
☐ Social interaction with peers ☐ Playing a game ☐ Going outside ☐ Video games
☐ iPad ☐ Helping teacher ☐ Reading ☐ Watching TV/video
☐ Going for a walk ☐ Extra free time
☐ Sensory activity (specify) _____
☐ Food (specify) _____
☐ Objects (specify) _____

2. Describe any other items, events, activities, or special interest topics/areas that are particularly motivating for the child: _____
_____
_____

Figure 3.8. Functional Behavior Assessment Interview Form *(cont.)*.

Additional Information

1.   What has been tried to address these behaviors?

Brief Description	What Happened?	How Long Was It Tried?

Summary of Data From SABC Forms and Functional Assessment Interview

Attach completed SABC Forms and provide an analysis of the data collected from those observation records and from the Functional Assessment Interview.

Student's Name: _____   Date:_____

Setting Events: Describe the biological, environmental, and/or social factors that appear to increase the likelihood that the interfering target behavior(s) will occur.

Biological, Social/Emotional Setting Events: _____
_____
_____

Environmental/Activity/Routine Setting Events: _____
_____
_____

Antecedents: Events that occur immediately before the behavior, triggering it: _____
_____
_____

Consequences: Events that occur after the behavior occurs, maintaining it: _____
_____
_____

Hypothesized Function(s) of the Target Behaviors

_____ engages in _____ when _____
   [Student's Name]   [Interfering Behavior]   [Antecedent]

because when s/he does _____. This is more likely to happen
                                       [Typical Consequence]

during_____ and/or when _____ have occurred.
          [Context]   [Setting Events]

Primary Function(s) of the Target Behavior:
_____
_____

Figure 3.8. **Functional Behavior Assessment Interview Form** *(cont.).*

The Functional Behavior Assessment (FBA) Interview Form consists of data from multiple sources. In addition to parent information, it includes information from ASD team members and a summary of the data obtained from SABC Charts.

Once the parent meeting has been conducted and the Functional Behavior Assessment Interview Form has been completed by a parent and by members of the ASD team, an intervention plan is created using Tier III supports and sometimes other supports delineated in collaboration with the ASD consultant. See Figure 3.9 for the Tier III Checklist of Strategies and Supports for Individual Students.

**Tier III
ASD Nest Program
Three-Tier Model**

Considerations for Tier III Intervention Supports

Most Tier III interventions are so intensive that they require frequent 1:1 implementation, consistent monitoring throughout the day, and ongoing consultation. Entry into any Tier III intervention must involve a meeting with a parent or guardian to gather and share information about supports and strategies to be used.

Sensory concerns: Tier III sensory interventions are intensive, individual supports that are implemented throughout the day and are developed and closely guided and monitored by the child's occupational therapist.

Behavior concerns: Movement from Tier II to Tier III requires that a complete functional behavior assessment (FBA) be done to derive a behavior intervention plan (BIP) that addresses the student's needs. Continued data collection on target behaviors is an essential component of Tier III interventions, which are all intensive and individualized. A behavior consultant and/or ASD Nest coach cluster teacher is involved throughout the FBA process and Tier III intervention implementation.

Social concerns: The team must agree that, based on a student's progress on his or her IEP goals, more individualized, intensive interventions are necessary. These supports should be introduced and closely monitored by the student's speech-language pathologist in collaboration with a Nest consultant.

Academic concerns: The team must complete the Tier III Academic Screening Form prior to implementing any Tier III strategies.

Tier III interventions offer intensive, individual support for students who continue to struggle with most grade-level expectations and who receive a rating of "1" (the lowest possible rating) in reading, writing, or math on their report card. Supplemental programs for decoding, math, or writing may be necessary to provide further support for students in this tier.

All data collected in considering and planning for Tier III interventions are saved in the student's file prior to implementing any of the strategies.

Figure 3.9. **Tier III Checklist for Individual Student Planning.**

Tier III

Tier III Strategies and Supports: Intensive, Individualized Interventions and Consultation

The strategies outlined below are used to guide the design of an intensive intervention plan for a student. Team members should identify the strategies across all four domains that are most relevant to help support the student. For each of those strategies, the team indicates whether it should be continued, modified, or added to the student's intervention plan by placing a checkmark in the appropriate column, in accordance with the key below. Comments on implementation recommendations may be added in the column on the right, entitled "Notes on Implementation."

Recommendations		
C	**M**	**A**
Continue current use of support	*Modify* existing support (Increase or decrease)	*Add* as a new support

Student Name: _____   **Date**:_____

Sensory Functioning & Self-Regulation Supports	Identify Strategies That Are Most Relevant			Notes on Implementation
	C	**M**	**A**	
1. Provide intensive use of individual, 1:1 sensory-based strategies throughout the day on a consistent schedule with consistent teacher support and data collection with monitoring by therapist to evaluate effectiveness.				
2. Provide individual <u>sensory schedule</u> with frequent breaks that require specific sensory input (e.g., proprioception, movement), teacher facilitation, and therapist supervision and monitoring.				
3. Implement break program with scheduled breaks every period.				
4. Provide prompted support/guidance for relaxation training throughout the day.				

Figure 3.9. **Tier III Checklist for Individual Student Planning** *(cont.).*

Behavioral Supports	Identify Strategies That Are Most Relevant			Notes on Implementation
	C	M	A	
1. Use individual task boards/mini-schedules with continued teacher guidance.				
2. Provide individualized planned priming for all tasks and events.				
3. Provide frequently scheduled teacher-supported break times throughout the day.				
4. Implement more intensive reinforcement system requiring frequent teacher monitoring.				
5. Consider using task simplification as a prevention strategy. (See item #2 under Academic/Social Supports below.)				

Social Supports	Identify Strategies That Are Most Relevant			Notes on Implementation
	C	M	A	
1. Preview all upcoming social events/activities (e.g., games, special activities, field trips) in 1:1 sessions run by a related service provider.				
2. Provide 1:1 proximity support during challenging social environments with the adult using self-talk/declarative language to facilitate student participation.				
3. Differentiate the use of social support vocabulary and incorporate activities/supports to both develop the concepts underlying the terminology and improve the student's understanding of social expectations.				

Academic/Curriculum Supports	Identify Strategies That Are Most Relevant			Notes on Implementation
	C	M	A	
1. Provide intensive, 1:1 support during lessons or activities/tasks.				
2. Modify significantly all content demands, work expectations, and curriculum/instructional pacing.				
3. Utilize supplemental programs to address specific academic weaknesses, such as decoding, computation, or fluency issues.				

Figure 3.9. **Tier III Checklist for Individual Student Planning** *(cont.).*

The behavior intervention plan embedded in the responses to the Tier III list of strategies and supports may be further clarified as well as expanded by using a form that organizes supports according to their primary function – prevention strategies, replacement strategies,and response strategies – which reflects the factors to be considered in providing intensive behavioral support. Figure 3.10 presents a Summary of Behavior Intervention Strategies Form that serves as a clearer version of the Behavior Intervention Plan (BIP).

Summary of Behavior Intervention Strategies

Student: _____ Date: _____
Target Behavior(s):_____

Prevention Strategies: These strategies involve intervening *prior* to the occurrence of impeding/interfering behavior.

- **Setting Events & Antecedent-Based Strategies** – Each modification is linked to the *Setting Events* and *Antecedents* identified.

Setting Events & Antecedents	Prevention Strategies

Replacement Strategies: These strategies involve *teaching* the student more effective and appropriate means of communicating, coping, and enhancing self-management skills.

Alternative Adaptive Behavior	Replacement Strategies

Response Strategies: These strategies modify the ways in which team members respond to both *interfering target behaviors* (decreasing the likelihood that they will occur) and *replacement behaviors* (increasing the likelihood that they will be used consistently).

Response Strategies	

Figure 3.10. Summary of Behavior Intervention Strategies Form.

Just as the implementation and outcomes of intervention plans designed for individual students at Tier I and Tier II must be monitored, so do the plans and outcomes for students receiving Tier III services. Therefore, about a month after the Tier III strategies have been implemented, a check-in takes place using a Tier III Check-In Form (the same form used in Tiers I and II except for the Tier III part of the title.) Figure 3.11 presents the Tier III Implementation Check-In Form.

Tier III Implementation Check-In Form

The first Tier III implementation check-in takes place approximately 3-4 weeks after the student's plan has been implemented. After that, if the student continues to make progress, check-in meetings can take place every 5-6 weeks.

Student: _____ **Date:** _____

Have the recommended strategies and supports been implemented? Describe when and how.

How did the student respond to the interventions? Have any improvements in the previously identified area(s) of concern taken place? If so, describe those changes by giving specific examples.

Next step(s) in supporting this student: Provide the team's recommendation(s) and identify the person(s) responsible for implementing them.

Figure 3.11. **Tier III Implementation Check-In Form.**

If at this time the student's functioning has still not shown signs of better approaching IEP goals and class/school expectations, other options are considered. A parent(s) or guardian is always included in exploring alternative educational experiences, such as a program with small, self-contained classes for students with ASD within the public school system or a non-public school for students with ASD that has small class sizes and a high ratio of professionals to students.

The steps for moving within and among Tiers I, II, and III are illustrated in the Sequence of Steps figures that follow.

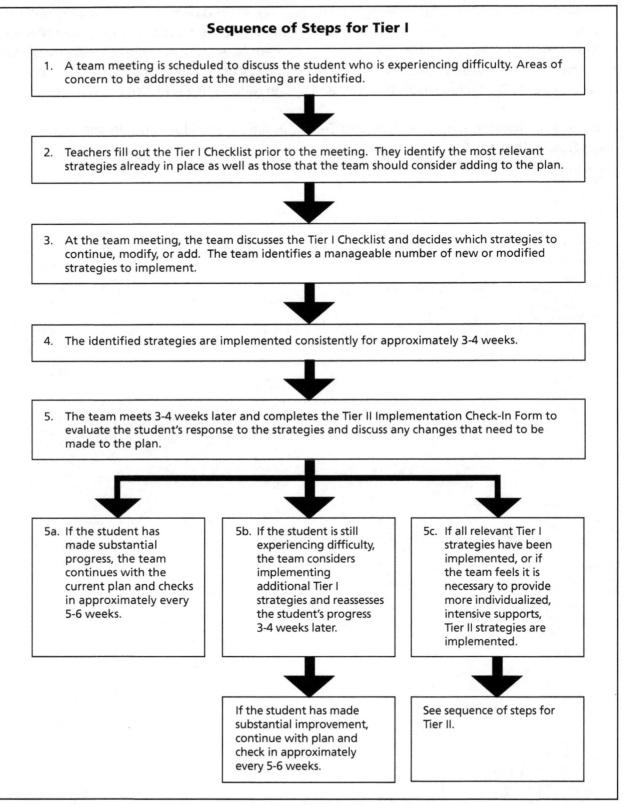

Sequence of Steps for Tier I

1. A team meeting is scheduled to discuss the student who is experiencing difficulty. Areas of concern to be addressed at the meeting are identified.

2. Teachers fill out the Tier I Checklist prior to the meeting. They identify the most relevant strategies already in place as well as those that the team should consider adding to the plan.

3. At the team meeting, the team discusses the Tier I Checklist and decides which strategies to continue, modify, or add. The team identifies a manageable number of new or modified strategies to implement.

4. The identified strategies are implemented consistently for approximately 3-4 weeks.

5. The team meets 3-4 weeks later and completes the Tier II Implementation Check-In Form to evaluate the student's response to the strategies and discuss any changes that need to be made to the plan.

5a. If the student has made substantial progress, the team continues with the current plan and checks in approximately every 5-6 weeks.

5b. If the student is still experiencing difficulty, the team considers implementing additional Tier I strategies and reassesses the student's progress 3-4 weeks later.

5c. If all relevant Tier I strategies have been implemented, or if the team feels it is necessary to provide more individualized, intensive supports, Tier II strategies are implemented.

If the student has made substantial improvement, continue with plan and check in approximately every 5-6 weeks.

See sequence of steps for Tier II.

Figure 3.12. Sequence of steps for Tier I.

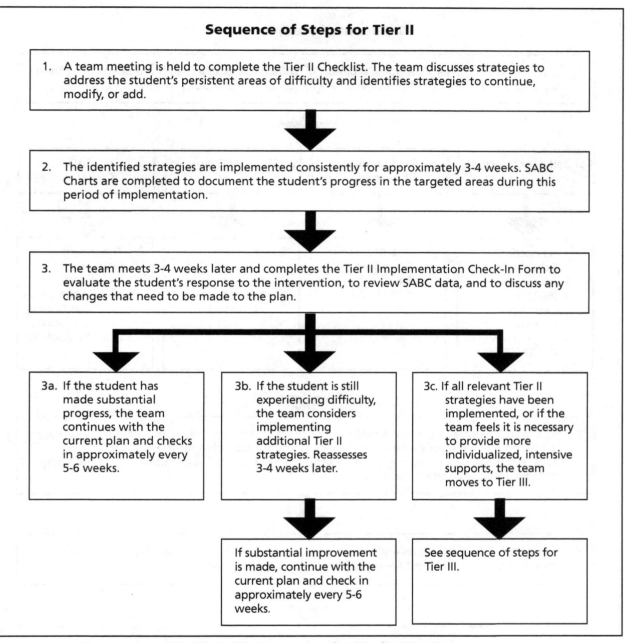

Figure 3.13. **Sequence of steps for Tier II.**

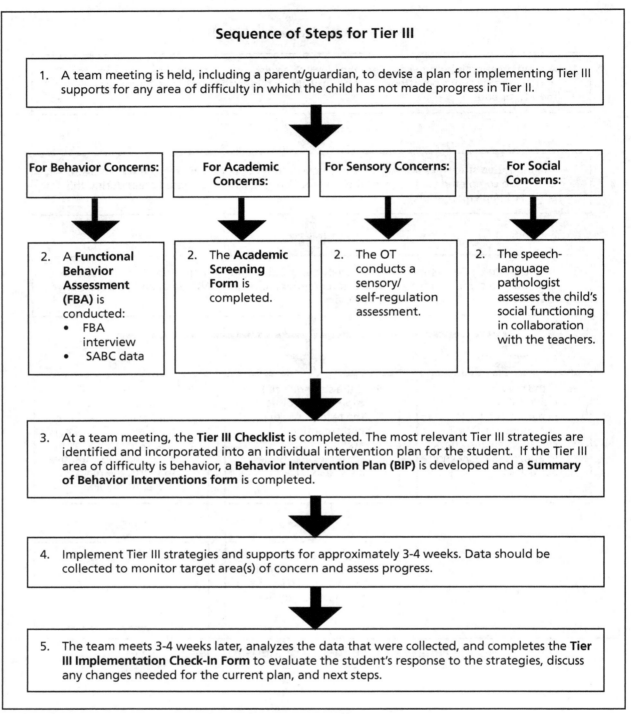

Sequence of Steps for Tier III

1. A team meeting is held, including a parent/guardian, to devise a plan for implementing Tier III supports for any area of difficulty in which the child has not made progress in Tier II.

For Behavior Concerns:

For Academic Concerns:

For Sensory Concerns:

For Social Concerns:

2. A **Functional Behavior Assessment (FBA)** is conducted:
   - FBA interview
   - SABC data

2. The **Academic Screening Form** is completed.

2. The OT conducts a sensory/self-regulation assessment.

2. The speech-language pathologist assesses the child's social functioning in collaboration with the teachers.

3. At a team meeting, the **Tier III Checklist** is completed. The most relevant Tier III strategies are identified and incorporated into an individual intervention plan for the student. If the Tier III area of difficulty is behavior, a **Behavior Intervention Plan (BIP)** is developed and a **Summary of Behavior Interventions form** is completed.

4. Implement Tier III strategies and supports for approximately 3-4 weeks. Data should be collected to monitor target area(s) of concern and assess progress.

5. The team meets 3-4 weeks later, analyzes the data that were collected, and completes the **Tier III Implementation Check-In Form** to evaluate the student's response to the strategies, discuss any changes needed for the current plan, and next steps.

Figure 3.14. Sequence of steps for Tier III.

Conclusion

The ASD Nest Three-Tier Model of Strategies and Supports is a valuable tool for helping teachers and other members of ASD Nest teams strengthen their planning and intervention efforts on behalf of students in the program. As such, the model serves as (a) an organizer of staff thinking and planning, (b) a reminder of the critical importance of positive environments and interactions, and (c) a tool for professional development. The model has also allowed almost all the students on the autism spectrum to be served in this inclusion program, so that they can be educated with their more typically developing peers. Despite such progress and success experiences, we have not become complacent, however. We continue striving every day to find additional ways for delivering the most effective educational services possible for these children.

Chapter 4

The Three-Tier System and the Classroom Guideposts in Action

Jamie Bleiweiss and Lauren Hough

This chapter illustrates the use of the class and individual student checklists in conjunction with the Classroom Guideposts. These illustrations are meant to further clarify the use of the checklists in the implementation process. The chapter includes the following examples:

- Use of the Tier I Classroom Checklist of Strategies and Supports for a second-grade class

- Use of the Tier I Checklist of Strategies and Supports for a student in the second-grade

- Use of the Tier II Checklist of Strategies and Supports for a student in the first grade

- Use of the Tier III Checklist of Strategies and Supports along with ancillary forms for a student in the third grade

The Tier I Classroom Checklist in Operation

Jane Howe, a consultant for the ASD Nest Program, conducted a 50-minute observation in a second-grade Nest classroom. The co-teaching team was a new partnership including Mr. Vasquez, an experienced special education teacher in the ASD Nest Program, and Ms. Moss, a general education teacher with one year of experience in first grade.

When Ms. Howe entered the classroom, the students were on the rug with the lights off, and Ms. Moss was leading the class in a movement activity without verbal directions. The students "read" her nonverbal clues and followed along. They appeared calm and focused and seemed to be enjoying the activity. During that time, Mr. Vasquez put out materials for the math centers that would be used after a group lesson on math. After two more minutes of the movement activity, Mr. Vasquez turned the lights on and moved the arrow on the class schedule to math, asking, "What's it time for?," to which the class responded, "Math time!" Ms. Moss highlighted for Aidan, one of the students with ASD who had not responded, "It's time for math! Remember during writing, we said that 'after writing we get to do math!' and you were so excited!" Aidan grinned and turned to the lesson chart.

The teachers team-taught the math lesson, reviewing four math concepts that the class had been working on all week: telling time to the quarter hour, measuring in inches, basic two-digit addition, and solving number stories. The teachers dropped their voices to a whisper to get the students' attention and then raised them to show how excited they were with certain topics. The students appeared to be engaged, and Mr. Vasquez gave students thumbs-up for participating. Molly, a student with ASD, crossed her arms and grumbled when another student was called on and "stole her answer," but she perked up when Ms. Moss highlighted that situation was a "brain match" (two or more students having the same idea at the same time) and modeled how to "kiss your hand and tap your head to kiss your brain" when that happens, praising them for their smart thinking.

The teachers then told the class that everyone would be practicing their math skills in centers and explained what to do at each of the four math centers. Ms. Moss reviewed which students were in the blue, red, green, and yellow groups, and described where each of those groups would start. Some of the students did not turn around to look at the centers to which the teachers were pointing while explaining this. Overlooking the nonverbal information conveyed in her pointing and failing to see exactly *where* they would be working and *what* they would be doing meant that some students missed critical information that could help them transition and begin their work independently with their classmates. After reviewing the groups and centers, the teachers told the students to "1, 2, 3, and GO!" to their centers.

Students rushed off, bumping into one another to be the first to reach their center. Michael, one of the students with ASD, sat down at the measurement center, looked at the worksheet, and put his head down. Andre, another Nest student in the class, moved to the break area without ever reaching his center. The teachers circulated around the room, checking to ensure that students were finding their assigned centers.

The clock center activity was new to the students, and Mr. Vasquez had to teach it before they could begin to work independently. Most of the students at the measurement center seemed to understand what to do and how to record their answers, but Michael continued to sit with his head down, making no move to begin. The students at the addition worksheet center were able to start independently, putting up foam board "office carrels" to give them some private work space, so Ms. Moss moved on to support the students in the number stories group.

Once the students had settled into their group's work, the teachers began to offer help to students who appeared to be struggling. For example, Mr. Vasquez said to Michael, "I noticed that your head has been down and you have not started working. I think you are telling me that you need help." In response, Michael mumbled that the worksheet was too hard and that no one was helping him. Mr. Vasquez pointed out that he knows when someone needs help if they raise their hand and that he was there now to offer any help Michael needed. Michael was easily able to continue working after Mr. Vasquez provided some quick clarification about the directions and praised him for his work on his first completed problem.

Ms. Moss heard the timer go off in the break area and went over to Andre to invite him to the number story center. Andre said he was upset. He didn't know which center he was supposed to go to, and he wanted to go to measurement first. Ms. Moss showed him that he was going to start in the number stories center with the rest of the blue group, and explained that his group was going to the measurement center next. This seemed to satisfy Andre, and he was able to start his work with some proximity support from Ms. Moss.

After a few more minutes, the teachers stopped the students and told them that it was time to rotate to their next center. Some students continued to work at their current centers, and Ms. Moss had to talk over their voices as well as the voice of Mr. Vasquez, who was asking individual students to stop working and listen to directions. During each transition to the next center, the voices of the students and their teachers became louder, and the sound level in the classroom became somewhat overwhelming. During the last center rotation, Mr. Vasquez called out, "What level should we all be using from the voice scale when we are working in centers?" Some students answered "2," others, "3." This interchange led to some lowering of student voice levels, but the teachers themselves did not lower their voice levels very much, even when working with individual students.

After the final math center rotation was completed, the teachers brought the students back to the rug and shared some highlights from the work they had observed during centers, and each student received a star on the classwide reinforcement system. Finally, Mr. Vasquez updated the class schedule, showing the students that math was over, adding, "And now it's time for (pause) …" to which the class yelled, "Lunch!"

■　■　■

Ms. Howe completed a Tier I Classroom Checklist of Strategies and Supports during and shortly after her observation.

Tier I
Classroom Checklist
ASD Nest Program
Three-Tier Model

Tier I Strategies and Supports for ASD Nest Classes

The Tier I Classroom Checklist is used by the ASD Nest consultant to ensure full implementation of the Tier I strategies of the ASD Nest Three-Tier Model. The ASD Nest consultant uses this tool to ensure that the strategies are being used consistently to support students. There is no expectation that every strategy will be implemented during all lessons and other activities in every classroom but rather that the strategies will be used frequently, whenever relevant, before more intensive individualized supports are pursued.

The Tier I strategies and supports listed in this checklist are divided into two levels, A & B, in each of the four domains (Sensory, Behavior, Social, Academic):

> **Level A** supports should <u>always</u> be present and readily observable during a 45- to 50-minute classroom visit.

> **Level B** supports are <u>additional</u> strategies that <u>may</u> be implemented in the classroom.

Directions for Using the Tier I Classroom Checklist:

1. Fill out class information requested at the top of the form on the next page.

2. Complete the checklist across all four domains as follows: For each item, indicate whether the strategy was **Observed** or **Not observed** by checking the appropriate box.

   ☐ **Observed** (for applicable items, indicate if it was used **"consistently"** or **"on occasion"**)

   ☐ **Not observed** (for applicable items, indicate **"missed opportunity"** and specify further in the Notes column)

3. Circle all Level A strategies that were either **Not observed** or were observed **"on occasion"** to identify the items that need further attention.

4. Meet with the teachers to highlight effective supports being used and to review a manageable number of Level A strategies and supports not yet implemented or implemented inconsistently. The ASD school team works with the teachers and the consultant to plan for more consistent use of the targeted Tier I strategies.

5. Follow up on implementation of suggested strategies and supports at the next classroom visit.

*Expanded definitions for underlined terms in the Tier I Classroom Checklist may be found in Chapter 3.

Figure 4.1. Tier I Strategies and Supports for All ASD Nest Classes.

Note. In the following, underlining is used to highlight key terms in a strategy. Boldface is used to draw attention to supports selected for an individual child.

Tier I	Classroom: <u>Ms. Moss & Mr. Vasquez</u> Subject(s)/Activities: <u>Math Workshop</u> Completed by: <u>Ms. Howe</u> Date & Time: <u>10/3/12; 11:40-12:30 pm</u>

Sensory Functioning & Self-Regulation Supports		Notes
LEVEL A: Supports that should *always* be present and observable in each 45- to 50-minute observation period:		
1. Classroom environment accommodates sensory sensitivities and prevents sensory overload.	☒ Observed ☐ Not observed	Calming and consistent colors; tennis balls on legs of chairs.
2. Arousing and calming activities are balanced across the period.	☒ Observed ☐ Not observed	Nice nonverbal movement series for relaxation before mini-lesson.
3. <u>Break area</u> is inviting, available for student use, and offers materials for calming.	☒ Observed ☐ Not observed	
4. Teachers modify voice volume appropriate to individual students and to the size of the group.	☒ Observed ☐ Consistently ☒ On occasion ☐ Not observed	Teacher I lowered voice after relaxation series before mini-lesson, but both teachers used loud voices when supporting individual students later on.
5. Opportunities are created for whole-class movement (e.g., movement break or transition between rug/desk).	☒ Observed ☐ Not observed: ☐ Missed opportunity	
LEVEL B: *Additional* support strategies that *may* be implemented:		
6. Relaxation activities are used to develop strategies for self-regulation (e.g., deep breathing, selected yoga movements).	☒ Observed ☐ Not observed: ☐ Missed opportunity	
7. <u>Sensory tools</u> are used by/available to students (e.g., work carrels, headphones, fidgets).	☒ Observed ☐ Not observed: ☐ Missed opportunity	Work carrels were used during independent work for some students (suggest keeping them where students can access them independently).

Figure 4.1. Tier I Strategies and Supports for All ASD Nest Classes *(cont.)*.

Behavioral Supports		Notes
LEVEL A: Supports that should *always* be present and observable in each 50-minute observation period:		
1. Classroom is organized to minimize visual distraction.	☒ Observed ☐ Not observed	Organized materials, minimal teacher clutter, bookcases covered.

2. Daily <u>class schedule</u> is displayed and referenced as a transition/refocusing support.	☒ Observed
	  ☐ Consistently
	  ☒ On occasion
	☐ Not observed
		Daily schedule was displayed, but very small – students could not read from their desks. Also, schedule was not correct or referenced between each period.

3. <u>Visual aids</u> and concrete examples are utilized to supplement verbal directions.	☐ Observed
	  ☐ Consistently
	  ☒ On occasion
	☒ Not observed
		All directions (3-4 steps) were verbal. Need to work on limiting number of steps and providing visual supports to supplement verbal directions.

4. Students are told what *to do* rather than what *not to do.*	☒ Observed
	  ☐ Consistently
	  ☒ On occasion
	☐ Not observed
		Nice positive language – clear behavioral expectations.

5. Clear, concise, concrete language is used to clarify expectations.	☒ Observed
	  ☐ Consistently
	  ☒ On occasion
	☐ Not observed
		Language and expectations are clear when given to group on the rug; become less clear when given to students at their desks.

6. Teachers "<u>catch students being good,</u>" providing behavior-specific praise.	☒ Observed
	  ☒ Consistently
	  ☐ On occasion
	☐ Not observed
		Nice language from both teachers – also tied to their classroom behavior system.

7. Appropriate behavior in peers is highlighted.	☒ Observed
	  ☒ Consistently
	  ☐ On occasion
	☐ Not observed	

8. <u>Classwide reinforcement system</u> with clear, concrete behavioral expectations is used	☒ Observed
	  ☐ Consistently
	  ☒ On occasion
	☐ Not observed
		Star system is in place; not clear exactly what students need to do to earn a star. Delivery seems somewhat random – not clear exactly what behaviors are being reinforced.

9. Upcoming activities/transitions/ expectations are previewed.	☒ Observed ☐ Not observed	
10. <u>5-Point Scales</u> are created and referenced to concretize abstract concepts (e.g., voice volume, level of control, size of a problem).	☒ Observed ☐ Not observed: ☐ Missed opportunity	5-Point Voice Scale is posted and teachers use language to clarify expectations.
11. Opportunities are provided for students to make choices.	☐ Observed ☒ Not observed	

Figure 4.1. **Tier I Strategies and Supports for All ASD Nest Classes** *(cont.).*

Behavioral Supports		Notes
LEVEL B: *Additional* support strategies that *may* be implemented:		
12. Visual <u>task sequencing boards</u> are used for routines and activities.	☐ Observed ☒ Not observed: 　☐ Missed opportunity	
13. Nurturing <u>peer buddies</u> are used to provide support.	☐ Observed ☒ Not observed: 　☐ Missed opportunity	
14. Student strengths and interests are incorporated into learning activities.	☐ Observed 　☐ Consistently 　☐ On occasion ☒ Not observed 　☒ Missed opportunity	Opportunity to incorporate student interests in modeling measurement lesson (How many inches do you think a subway seat is? How long do you think our class lizard is?).
15. <u>Proximity control/signal interference</u> is used as a prevention strategy.	☐ Observed ☒ Not observed 　☐ Missed opportunity	
16. "<u>Looking forward to</u>" approach is used to help students anticipate upcoming, preferred activities.	☐ Observed ☒ Not observed 　☐ Missed opportunity	
17. <u>Visual timers</u> are used for classroom transitions and activities to clearly display length/passage of time.	☐ Observed ☒ Not observed 　☒ Missed opportunity	Auditory timer was used; students could not monitor passage of time because they could not see it from their desks.

Social Supports		Notes
LEVEL A: Supports that should *always* be present and observable in each 50-minute observation period:		
1. <u>Nonverbal language</u> is used (e.g., eye gaze, gestures, facial expressions).	☒ Observed 　☐ Consistently 　☒ On occasion ☐ Not observed	Used while students were together on the carpet, relied on verbal only when students were at their desks; made independent work time language-heavy.
2. Strategies and supports that foster a classroom community/team are used (e.g., "we" language, table names, room themes, photos of shared experiences).	☐ Observed 　☐ Consistently 　☐ On occasion ☒ Not observed	Classroom is positive, but this could be a powerful thing to work on to make the students more engaged and invested in their classroom experiences!

Figure 4.1. Tier I Strategies and Supports for All ASD Nest Classes *(cont.).*

Social Supports		Notes

3. Indirect prompts (e.g., declarative statements or gestures) are used.	☐ Observed
	   ☐ Consistently
	   ☐ On occasion
	☒ Not observed
		Language is all imperatives/ questions; declarative language could increase student problem solving and novel, spontaneous commenting.

4. Students are given extra time to process and respond to language in social situations (e.g., transitioning, talking to a peer/teacher at desks).	☒ Observed
	   ☒ Consistently
	   ☐ On occasion
	☐ Not observed	

5. Experience-sharing language is used (e.g., celebrating, labeling the moment, teamwork).	☐ Observed ☒ Not observed	Similar to #2 in this section; this is absent and would be a nice addition to this community.
6. Teachers foster social engagement (e.g., building anticipation and excitement, remembering shared experiences).	☒ Observed ☐ Not observed	This was particularly evident during the lesson.
LEVEL B: *Additional* support strategies that *may* be implemented:		
7. Declarative language is used to invite experience-sharing.	☐ Observed ☒ Not observed ☒ Missed opportunity	
8. Self-talk is used to model Social Thinking® (Winner, 2005) and problem solving.	☐ Observed ☒ Not observed ☒ Missed opportunity	There were some nice opportunities to do this to model students gathering materials for independent work.
9. Basic Social Thinking® (Winner, 2005) language, *appropriate* for the grade, is used (e.g., flexibility, thinking about me/you© (Winner, 2007), listening with your whole body).	☐ Observed ☒ Not observed ☒ Missed opportunity	None of the social vocabulary was used during this period.
10. Small-group teamwork/problem-solving experiences are facilitated, providing adult support, using developmentally appropriate Social Thinking® (Winner, 2005) language and strategies.	☐ Observed ☒ Not observed ☒ Missed opportunity	Lots of opportunities for this during math games (who goes first, what if we are missing a piece, what if partners disagree? etc.).
11. Role-play is used with the whole class/ small groups to prepare for a new/difficult situation (e.g., fire drill, working with a partner, playing a math game).	☐ Observed ☒ Not observed ☐ Missed opportunity	
12. Social narratives and cartooning are used.	☐ Observed ☒ Not observed ☒ Missed opportunity	Many students were frustrated with work, and NONE independently asked for help – waited for teacher to offer. Great thing to address as a class.

Figure 4.1. **Tier I Strategies and Supports for All ASD Nest Classes** *(cont.).*

Academic/Curriculum Supports		Notes
LEVEL A: Supports that should *always* be present and observable in each 50-minute observation period:		
1. Teachers use variety of <u>co-teaching styles</u> (e.g., one teach-one assist, parallel teaching).	☒ Observed ☐ Not observed	
2. Mini-lessons are structured to promote active engagement, to assess mastery, and to help teachers differentiate their instruction. Mini-lessons contain (a) clear teaching point, (b) modeling, (c) guided student practice, (d) independent student practice, and (e) student share.	☐ Observed ☒ Not observed	No guided practice, so teachers missed that many students were confused; meant many needed help at desks.

3. Lessons are well-planned, and all materials related to the lesson and student work are ready and easily accessible.	☒ Observed
	  ☐ Consistently
	  ☒ On occasion
	☐ Not observed	

4. General visuals are used to clarify expectations and academic concepts during lessons and individual/group work times.	☒ Observed
	  ☒ Consistently
	  ☐ On occasion
	☐ Not observed	

5. Extra time is provided to students for processing and responding to oral communication.	☒ Observed
	  ☒ Consistently
	  ☐ On occasion
	☐ Not observed	

6. Directions for independent work are clear and concise. The number of steps in directions is limited, considering student age as well as language processing and cognitive levels.	☒ Observed
	  ☐ Consistently
	  ☒ On occasion
	☐ Not observed
		Clear when given to group on the rug, less clear when given to students sitting at their desks.

7. Pace of the lesson is appropriate for the students in the class.	☒ Observed ☐ Not observed	
8. The amount of independent work is appropriate for the students' grade and level of academic readiness.	☒ Observed ☐ Not observed	
9. Seating is planned strategically to facilitate <u>peer support</u>.	☐ Observed ☒ Not observed	Teachers provided all of the support; no established peer buddies.
10. Expectations for what students should do when they are finished with independent work are clear.	☒ Observed ☐ Not observed	Chart in front of room with rotating options of "What to do when I'm through …"

Figure 4.1. Tier I Strategies and Supports for All ASD Nest Classes *(cont.)*.

Academic/Curriculum Supports		Notes
LEVEL B: *Additional* support strategies that *may* be implemented:		
11. Complex academic activities are broken down (<u>task analysis</u>) to clarify and enumerate component steps and sequences.	☐ Observed ☒ Not observed ☒ Missed opportunity	Independent work had many steps, including materials to gather. Task analysis would have been helpful.
12. Manipulatives are used to clarify concepts and increase active engagement.	☐ Observed ☒ Not observed ☐ Missed opportunity	
13. Presentation of academic activities/tasks is modified to incorporate students' interests, strengths, or learning styles.	☐ Observed ☒ Not observed ☒ Missed opportunity	
14. Supports for asking for help are used.	☐ Observed ☒ Not observed ☒ Missed opportunity	Supports for asking for help are needed for many students in the class.
15. Graphic organizers are used for organizing, planning, and reflecting.	☐ Observed ☒ Not observed ☐ Missed opportunity	
16. Flexible small groups are used for differentiating instruction.	☐ Observed ☒ Not observed ☒ Missed opportunity	One teacher could have kept students on the rug who were still confused, reviewed teaching point and started them off before sending them back to work.
17. New, challenging material and/or content is previewed prior to instruction.	☐ Observed ☒ Not observed ☐ Missed opportunity	
18. Students are given the opportunity to work in small groups with the necessary supports.	☒ Observed ☐ Not observed ☐ Missed opportunity	
19. Whole-class response strategies are used in lessons (e.g., slates).	☐ Observed ☒ Not observed ☐ Missed opportunity	
20. Timers are used for independent work time cuing (by teachers).	☐ Observed ☒ Not observed ☒ Missed opportunity	Visual timer with sound would be helpful to encourage student time management.

Figure 4.1. Tier I Strategies and Supports for All ASD Nest Classes *(cont.).*

After the observation, Ms. Howe met with the teachers to discuss what she saw during her observation, using the Tier I Classroom Checklist to guide her feedback. Many of the Tier I strategies in Level A were in place in the classroom, including a daily class schedule that was referenced multiple times, nonverbal language activities, behavior-specific praise, and prepared lesson materials to prevent down-time.

Then Ms. Howe went on to identify the following Level A supports that could have been used more consistently, specifically the following:

- **Modulate voice levels – both teachers and students.** This was done very well during the whole-group activities early in the observation period but not during the center activities. The teachers can work on modifying their voice volume depending on the size of the group they are addressing and the format (e.g., individual support vs. whole-class directions). Use of the Incredible Five-Point Scale and teacher modeling of different voice levels appropriate for communicating with individuals and groups could also have been implemented more consistently.

- **Use visual aids to supplement verbal directions.** This would have been especially helpful for complex activities like rotating centers. A visual chart could have been created for each group to show the sequence of centers to which students would be going.

- **Use clear, concrete language to clarify expectations** during transitions, with additional support provided through modeling. One group could have served as a transition model for the other three groups as the students in that group moved from the rug through each step of the transition process to their centers, with a teacher describing what they were doing and how they were doing it.

- **Support and foster a classroom community** by capturing shared experiences with photographs. To do so, take a few minutes during center activities to take pictures of students working together, sharing materials, helping one another, and interacting in other positive ways.

- **Structure mini-lessons to include modeling and guided practice** to ensure that you can see who is ready to go off to work somewhat independently, and who needs more practice before leaving the rug area.

- **Use task analysis to break down tasks into clear, component steps.** This is a Level B academic strategy that the team could work on to break down multistep academic tasks after addressing the Level A strategies listed above.

Ms. Howe and the teachers discussed how these supports could be implemented in the classroom and how they could be used to benefit not only the students with ASD but other classmates as well. The teachers estimated that it might take two or three weeks to fully implement these changes and begin to see the results of their efforts. They agreed that it would be a good idea if Ms. Howe would check back at her visit later that month.

Later that week, Ms. Howe sent a follow-up email to the teachers thanking them for their work and for taking the time to meet with her after the observation. The teachers wrote back immediately to let her know that they had started implementing the recommended strategies and were already meeting with some success.

The Tier I Checklist of Strategies and Supports for Individual Students

Kayla: Tier I Case Study

Kayla, a second-grade student in the ASD Nest Program, adores coming to school and looks forward to Wednesday afternoons when she gets to go to art class and draw pictures of fantasy animals, which are her special interest. Pictures of unicorns, fairies, and dragons cover her folders and notebooks, and she has a seemingly limitless number of stories at her fingertips in which these animals embark on quests and adventures. Kayla's creativity and enthusiasm are easily channeled into art class, but she has a hard time in lessons that are more academically focused and structured.

Her teachers describe her as "dreamy" and "off in her own world" during lessons. Even when Kayla is asked a question on material with which she is familiar, she rarely knows the answer and sometimes doesn't even know what question was asked. Moreover, she never raises her hand to ask or answer a question in class.

Kayla's teachers thought that having one teacher sit next to her on the rug might provide a needed support, allowing the teacher to refocus her when her attention was waning. However, they found that having somebody sit next to her was sometimes a further distraction, as she would turn to the teacher on the rug, seemingly unaware of the lesson that was going on, and ask the teacher, "What is *your* favorite fairy color?" Her teachers became increasingly concerned about the content in the class lessons that Kayla was missing.

Although Kayla transitioned easily from the rug to her desk for independent work time, and was organized and meticulous in gathering the materials she saw her classmates collecting for their assignments, when it was time to begin her work, Kayla presented a different picture. She would look around the classroom, start conversations with her tablemates, and get up to ask the teachers about their favorite animals and if they thought that dragons were real. Further, she did not notice when her classmates or teachers were confused about her off-topic conversations during work time.

Writing was the task that Kayla had the most trouble starting independently. When her teachers spoke to her, she seemed to have many ideas about what she could write; however, she was reluctant to write about topics she found "boring," like stories about her life, and instead wanted to tell her teachers stories from her imagination. When her teachers gave her the freedom to write about whatever she wanted, she still had a hard time organizing her thinking and remembering the writing strategies taught in the group lessons that week. Kayla's teachers began to be very concerned about her falling behind in academics, as the lessons were becoming more challenging and the writing demands were increasing.

Kayla's teachers brought their observations to the team at their next case conference, sharing their concerns about Kayla's level of attention, her off-topic comments, and her inability to start and complete independent work at her desk. The team completed a Tier I Checklist of Strategies and Supports for Individual Students, shown in Figure 4.2, to assess the current level of support being provided to Kayla.

Tier I
ASD Nest Program
Three-Tier Model

Tier I Checklist for Individual Student Planning: *Relevant for All Nest Classes*

This individual student form is to be completed by the student's teachers and other members of the school team for planning more effective use of Tier I strategies. Team members identify the strategies across all four domains that are most relevant to help support the student. For each of the strategies, indicate whether it should be continued, modified, or added to the student's intervention plan by placing a checkmark in the appropriate column, in accordance with the key below. Comments on implementation recommendations may be added in the column on the right, entitled "Notes on Implementation."

Recommendations		
C	**M**	**A**
Continue current use of support	**Modify** existing support (Increase or decrease)	**Add** as a new support

Student Name: Kayla, 2nd grade   ***Date:*** October 4, 2013

Sensory Functioning & Self-Regulation Supports	Identify Strategies That Are Most Relevant			Notes on Implementation
	C	**M**	**A**	
1. Modify classroom environments to accommodate sensory sensitivities and prevent sensory overload.				
2. Balance arousing and calming activities across the day.				
3. Create and promote the use of a <u>break area</u> that contains calming materials for self-regulation.				
4. Monitor teacher voice volume so that it is appropriate to individuals in the class and to the size of the group.				
5. Utilize whole-class movement activities throughout the day.				
6. Use classroom relaxation activities throughout the day.				
7. **Make <u>sensory tools</u> available, as appropriate (e.g., work carrels, headphones, fidgets).**			✔	Work carrel; post task analysis, include picture of interest (e.g., dragon).

Figure 4.2. Tier I Checklist for Individual Student Planning.

Behavioral Supports	Identify Strategies That Are Most Relevant			Notes on Implementation
	C	M	A	
1. Display daily <u>class schedule</u> and reference frequently.				
2. Organize classroom to minimize visual distraction.				
3. Utilize <u>visual aids</u> and concrete examples to supplement verbal directions.				
4. Provide opportunities for students to make choices throughout the day.				
5. Incorporate student strengths & interests into learning activities.		✔		Capitalize on opportunities to incorporate her interests to increase motivation.
6. Tell students what *to do* rather than what *not to do*.				
7. Use clear, concise, concrete language to clarify expectations.				
8. **"<u>Catch them being good</u>" and provide behavior-specific praise.**	✔			Find more opportunities to provide behavior-specific praise when she is attending, participating, and starting work independently.
9. Use <u>proximity control/signal interference</u> preventively.				
10. Highlight appropriate behavior in peers.				
11. Anticipate upcoming preferred activities ("<u>looking forward to</u>" approach).				
12. Preview upcoming activities/transitions/expectations.				
13. Use and refer to the <u>Incredible 5-Point Scale</u> to concretize abstract concepts.				
14. **Use visual <u>task sequencing boards</u> for routines and activities.**		✔		She has general writing checklist. Add checklist created with teacher during lessons for independent work.
15. **Select nurturing <u>peer buddies</u> to provide support.**			✔	Capitalize on positive response to peer support; match with peer buddy at her writing table.
16. Use classwide <u>visual timers</u> for transitions and activities to indicate activity duration.				
17. Implement <u>classwide reinforcement system</u> (e.g., reward chart) that has clear, concrete expectations, spelling out specific behaviors/skills to be reinforced.				

Figure 4.2. Tier I Checklist for Individual Student Planning *(cont.).*

Social Supports	Identify Strategies That Are Most Relevant			Notes on Implementation
	C	M	A	
1. Use <u>nonverbal language</u> and communication to promote referencing and engagement.				
2. Use strategies and supports that foster a classroom community/team (e.g., "we" language, table names, room themes, photos of shared experiences).				
3. Foster <u>social engagement</u> (e.g., building anticipation, encoding and revisiting shared memories).				
4. Provide students with extra time to process and respond to language in social situations.				
5. Use experience-sharing language (e.g., <u>celebrating</u>, <u>labeling the moment</u>, teamwork).				
6. Use <u>declarative language</u> to foster experience-sharing.				
7. Use <u>self-talk</u> to model Social Thinking® (Winner, 2005), language, and problem solving.			✔	Self-talk modeling steps to help organize her thinking and highlight other people's thinking.
8. Use indirect prompts such as declarative statements, gestures, eye gaze, and physical proximity to enhance social awareness.				
9. Use basic Social Thinking® (Winner, 2005) language *appropriate* for the grade (e.g., <u>flexibility</u>, <u>thinking about me/you</u>© (Winner, 2007), <u>listening with your whole body</u>).				
10. Facilitate teamwork and problem-solving experiences in small groups using developmentally appropriate Social Thinking® (Winner, 2005) language and strategies.				
11. Lead whole class/small groups in <u>role-playing</u> new/difficult situations.				
12. <u>Social narratives</u> and/or <u>cartooning</u> are used to support some students to highlight the social aspects of a situation.				

Academic/Curriculum Supports	Identify Strategies That Are Most Relevant			Notes on Implementation
	C	M	A	
1. Utilize a variety of <u>co-teaching styles</u> (e.g., one teach-one assist; parallel group).		✔		Using one teach and one observe; add one teach, one assist on carpet creating checklist and monitoring for understanding.
2. Collaboratively plan lessons and prepare all necessary materials to ensure that everything is ready and easily accessible.				

Figure 4.2. **Tier I Checklist for Individual Student Planning** *(cont.).*

Academic/Curriculum Supports	Identify Strategies That Are Most Relevant			Notes on Implementation
	C	M	A	
3. Use mini-lesson structure for academic lesson, providing a clear teaching point, modeling, facilitating guided practice, allowing for independent student practice, and then reconvening for a share after independent/group work.				
4. Preview new, challenging material and/or content prior to instruction.				
5. Use flexible small groups to differentiate instruction.				
6. Plan seating strategically to facilitate peer support.			✔	Peers at her table could help check that K gets started at desk (peer buddy).
7. Allow extra time for processing and responding to oral communication.				
8. Provide clear, concise directions for independent work, limiting the number of steps in directions and considering student age, cognitive, and language processing levels.				
9. Use a variety of visuals to clarify lesson, individual, and group work expectations/academic concepts.			✔	Needs checklist for independent work; 2nd teacher can create during lesson with her on white board.
10. Modify presentation of academic activities/tasks to incorporate interests, strengths, or learning styles.			✔	Use interests; incorporate interests into subjects (writing topics) and lessons.
11. Use graphic organizers for organizing, planning, and reflecting.				
12. Use manipulatives across lessons, whenever relevant, to clarify concepts and increase active engagement.				
13. Use whole-class response strategies in lessons (e.g., slates).				
14. Task analyze complex academic activities to clarify component steps and sequences.			✔	See #9 above; create with her during lessons, she can check off independently at desk.
15. Provide supports to facilitate students' asking for help.				
16. Utilize timers for independent work time cuing.				
17. Pace lessons and amount of independent work required so that it is appropriate for the students' grade and level of academic readiness.				
18. Provide clear expectations for what students should do when they are finished with their independent work.				
19. Provide opportunities for students to work in small groups with the necessary supports.				

Figure 4.2. **Tier I Checklist for Individual Student Planning** *(cont.).*

During the discussion about the supports currently in place in the classroom, the team identified a number of strategies from which team members felt Kayla was benefiting. Kayla checks the daily class schedule several times a day and likes being able to find out when there are any changes to the schedule as well as what the next activity will be. She loves it when the teachers compliment her for being a good listener and for helping her classmates. She also responds well to peers when they remind her about what she should be doing, and she looks to them for help if she is confused. When the teachers write the directions for the independent work on the board, Kayla references them frequently and is more likely to be on task.

As the team dug deeper into some of the tasks that posed particular challenges for Kayla, they discovered that they had never explained to Kayla *why* the second teacher was sitting on the rug with her during lessons. The team thought that if they clarified for Kayla that the teacher was sitting next to her to help make sure that she was thinking about and understanding the lesson, maybe Kayla would be more likely to stay focused on the lesson.

The team also thought that some visual supports might help organize Kayla. Because Kayla made good use of directions for tasks that were written on the board, they thought it would be helpful to go a step further and create a checklist during each writing lesson that Kayla could use as a reference for the independent work that she and the other students were expected to do following each group lesson. That way, when Kayla got back to her desk for writing, she would know what she had to do **first** (date her journal entry), **second** (think of a time when she felt "curious," for example), and then **third** (write her story in complete sentences thinking about *who, what, where,* and *what happened)*. This checklist could also be displayed for the whole class to reference during independent work. Creating the checklist during the lesson might help Kayla stay more connected during the lesson itself, reinforcing the concepts being taught and modeled. The team also thought that a work carrel might help Kayla block out visual distractions, and brainstormed how they could post her checklist inside the carrel for easy referencing.

As Kayla responded well to compliments from the teachers for appropriate behavior, the team felt that the teachers should offer such behavior-based compliments as often as Kayla's actions allowed. In addition, as Kayla responded well to peers, looking toward them when she was confused but also offering them help, the team believed that a peer buddy might be a worthwhile additional strategy to offer.

The teachers also discussed ways to incorporate Kayla's special interests into the lessons to make her more motivated to participate. The speech-language pathologist suggested ways to incorporate animals that Kayla was interested in into word problems, and the teachers discussed finding more books for read-alouds that included fantasy characters that all the students might find interesting. For example, a motivating picture of a dragon could be posted in the work carrel as an added incentive.

Another issue discussed by the team was the language to use if Kayla approached them during academic work time to talk about something that was not relevant to the current activity. In addition to redirecting Kayla back to her desk and checklist, the speech-language pathologist suggested that the teachers and other team members respond with a statement explaining *their* thinking about her off-task comments or questions while also validating her thoughts: "Kayla, I know that *you* are thinking about dragons, but right now *I* am thinking writing. I'm excited about the amazing story that you are going to write when you get started with #2 on your checklist." Clarifying for her what others are thinking about could help Kayla become more connected to the class and provide further support to draw her back to the assigned task.

The team agreed that Kayla's writing challenges may not be fully addressed by the checklist and the language responses on what others are thinking, so they asked the teachers to sit with Kayla a few times during her writing assignments to find out if she could tell her story orally, draw the parts of her story, and/or write a story if they gave her a bank of words that they knew she would be using after she explained her story. The teachers also thought that allowing Kayla to write a fantasy story after she completed a story on the lesson topic might serve as an individual reinforcement that would increase her motivation. They agreed to spend the next week implementing these strategies and learning more about her skills as a writer.

At the end of the conference, the team decided to implement the following strategies and supports:

- **Use a variety of co-teaching styles: Implement a one teach-one support model** so that one teacher can provide support for Kayla on the rug while the other teacher leads the group lesson.

- **Use a task analysis checklist:** Created during the lesson listing what Kayla and the other students would need to do when she and the others got back to their seats for independent work. Make sure that Kayla understands how to use the checklist effectively as she completes independent work.

- **Use sensory tools:** Create a **work carrel** to block out visual distractions.

- **Incorporate Kayla's interests:** Include and teach through Kayla's interests, whenever possible.

- **Increase the frequency of praise** provided to Kayla whenever she shows improvement in attending/participating in group learning experiences or starts working on independent academic tasks with less delay.

- **Model and highlight the thinking of others:** Share with Kayla that you are thinking about the lesson if she asks you an off-topic question and redirect her to the task at hand.

- **Identify a possible peer buddy for Kayla:** Select a nurturing and competent peer who can serve as a role model and offer assistance to Kayla when she appears to be confused or not on task; provide guidance to that peer on how to respond to Kayla's questions about her fantasy interests.

- **Increase individual support during writing:** Provide 1:1 support during writing for the next week to identify what types of writing supports Kayla seems to respond to best.

The team decided to check back on how Kayla was doing in about three weeks. At this follow-up meeting, the team completed a Tier I Implementation Check-in Form (see Figure 4.3).

Tier I Implementation Check-In Form

The first Tier I implementation check-in should take place approximately 3-4 weeks after the student's plan has been implemented. After that, if the student continues to make progress, check-in meetings can take place every 5-6 weeks.

Student: _____Kayla_____ **Date:** _Thursday October 25, 2013_____

Have the recommended strategies and supports (additions/modifications) been implemented?

All of the recommended strategies based on the initial completion of the Tier I Checklist had been implemented by the team when they all checked in again after three weeks.

How did the student respond to the interventions? Have any improvements in the previously identified areas of concern taken place? If so, describe those changes by giving specific examples.

The team agreed that Kayla had made some nice progress with the Tier I strategies put in place in the classroom. More structured teacher support during lessons on the rug helped her focus, and creating a checklist with her during the lesson on both the content of the lesson and what her job would be during independent work helped sustain her attention and increased her ability to start her work independently at her desk. The teachers also incorporated her interests in the language of the checklist and in the lesson content, whenever possible, which was a great motivator for her and also celebrated her wonderful creativity. Kayla continued to respond to praise from her teachers when they noticed her focusing and using her strategies. During transitions, Kayla responded to teachers' highlighting when she was thinking about dragons while others seemed to be thinking about their work. She started to consider alternate times when other people might want to talk with her about her special interest (saying, "OK, we'll talk about dragons at lunch, then."). When Kayla worked at her desk, she used her "unicorn stable" work carrel and posted her checklist inside for easy reference. She also sometimes used her checklist to help peers when they did not know what to do. If her tablemates noticed that she was having trouble getting started on her work or setting up her carrel, they helped her, and she seemed happy to receive this peer support.

Next step in supporting this student: Provide the team's recommendation(s).

At this follow-up meeting, the team decided to continue the Tier I strategies that had been put in place as they seemed to be addressing many of Kayla's challenges with focus, knowing what to do during independent work, and noticing what others are thinking about during different times in the day. The team agreed that while Kayla was making great progress, writing was still a struggle for her. She was requiring a lot of l:l support and was having trouble using her unbelievable creativity during writing tasks. They decided to consider some Tier 2 academic strategies to help support her in writing and to work closely with the OT when designing additional strategies to help Kayla in this area.

Figure 4.3. **Tier I Implementation Check-In Form.**

The teachers found that supporting Kayla on the carpet during lessons and creating a checklist with her that she could use during her independent work time was very helpful in terms of keeping her focused and helping her know what she needed to do when she got back to her desk. When she did wander during independent work times and tried to talk about dragons, her teachers highlighted what they were thinking about, and she returned to her desk, saying, "OK, we'll talk about dragons at lunch then." Kayla was able to start her independent work more easily during reading and math and even helped other students at her table when they were confused about what to do by showing them her checklist.

But writing continued to be a struggle. Although she had her checklist for writing, Kayla still did not independently begin writing tasks, especially those that required that she write realistic fiction or nonfiction. The teachers and OT noticed that Kayla was able to verbally tell a realistic fiction story if given prompt cards with "Who," "Where," "When," and "What happened?" However, she had a hard time getting her ideas down on paper. But if her teacher wrote her ideas while she dictated, Kayla came up with complete stories with a surprising level of detail that far surpassed what she could produce independently. The team felt that Kayla's writing challenges demanded more individualized supports and decided that they would look into Tier II academic strategies to address her weaknesses in writing. The team agreed to think about additional strategies particularly relevant to writing problems before the next case conference on Kayla.

The Tier II Checklist of Strategies and Supports for Individual Students

Jonah: Tier II Case Study

Jonah, an incredibly bright student in a first-grade ASD Nest classroom, had a strong desire to share his in-depth knowledge about comic books with his classmates. However, his teachers began to notice that for several weeks, he appeared to become increasingly anxious when presented with new and challenging tasks and was more frequently engaging in angry outbursts that caused significant disruption to the classroom. They also noted that while Jonah was at or above grade level in most academic subjects, he had begun to produce less work, as the frequency of his meltdowns and disruptive behaviors had considerably increased. When Jonah made an error on an assignment, encountered a task that was difficult for him, was not the first student to finish a task, or did not win a game, he became highly agitated and began to anxiously pace back and forth near his desk, repeatedly bang pencils or throw nearby objects onto the floor, and made repeated negative comments and complaints aloud, which greatly disrupted his classmates. According to his teachers, these behaviors often led to more intense and lengthy meltdowns that significantly impeded his participation in the classroom.

Jonah's parents reported that he was having trouble coping with changes in circumstances at home as they were going through a divorce, and he had been spending greater amounts of time with the babysitter after school and in the evenings in recent weeks. The school-based ASD Nest team held a case conference meeting to address Jonah's areas of difficulty. They completed a Tier I Checklist of Strategies and Supports for Individual Students (shown in Figure 4.4) to assess the current level of support they were offering Jonah and to identify additional strategies to help support him better throughout the day.

Tier I Checklist for Individual Student Planning: *Relevant for All Nest Classes*

This individual student form is to be completed by the student's teachers and other members of the school team for planning more effective use of Tier I strategies. Team members identify the strategies across all four domains that are most relevant to help support the student. For each of those strategies, indicate whether it should be continued, modified, or added to the student's intervention plan by placing a checkmark in the appropriate column, in accordance with the key below. Comments on implementation recommendations may be added in the column on the right, entitled "Notes on Implementation."

Recommendations		
C	**M**	**A**
Continue *current use of support*	**Modify** *existing support (Increase or decrease)*	**Add** *as a new support*

Student Name: Jonah O.   *Date:* Tuesday, January 17, 2013

Sensory Functioning & Self-Regulation Supports	Identify Strategies That Are Most Relevant			Notes on Implementation
	C	**M**	**A**	
1. Modify classroom environments to accommodate sensory sensitivities and prevent sensory overload.				
2. Balance arousing and calming activities across the day.				
3. **Create and promote the use of a <u>break area</u> that contains calming materials for self-regulation.**		✔		Increase frequency of encouraging him to take a break, prior to escalation of frustration level.
4. Monitor teacher voice volume so that it is appropriate to individuals in the class and to the size of the group.				
5. Utilize whole-class movement activities throughout the day.				
6. Use classroom relaxation activities throughout the day.				
7. Make <u>sensory tools</u> available, as appropriate (e.g., work carrels, headphones, fidgets).				

Figure 4.4. Tier I Checklist for Individual Student Planning.

Behavioral Supports	Identify Strategies That Are Most Relevant			Notes on Implementation
	C	M	A	
1. Display daily <u>class schedule</u> and reference frequently.				
2. Organize classroom to minimize visual distraction.				
3. Utilize <u>visual aids</u> and concrete examples to supplement verbal directions.	✔			Use visual representations to clarify instructions – make things more concrete for him.
4. Provide opportunities for students to make choices throughout the day.	✔			Increase motivation by giving him choice – making opportunities.
5. Incorporate student strengths & interests into learning activities.				
6. Tell students what to do rather than what not to do.				
7. Use clear, concise, concrete language to clarify expectations.				
8. "<u>Catch them being good</u>" and provide behavior-specific praise.		✔		Increase frequency of praising specific actions/ behaviors; he is very responsive to praise & positive attention from adults.
9. Use <u>proximity control</u>/<u>signal interference</u> preventively.	✔			Teachers are positioned near Jonah to redirect him when he begins verbalizations.
10. Highlight appropriate behavior in peers.				
11. Anticipate upcoming preferred activities ("<u>looking forward to</u>" approach).				
12. Preview upcoming activities/transitions/expectations.	✔			Briefly review steps in upcoming activity or transition to help him more clearly understand what is expected.
13. Use and refer to the <u>Incredible 5-Point Scale</u> to concretize abstract concepts.				
14. Use visual <u>task sequencing boards</u> for routines and activities.				
15. Select nurturing <u>peer buddies</u> to provide support.				
16. Use classwide <u>visual timers</u> for transitions and activities to indicate activity duration.				
17. Implement <u>classwide reinforcement system</u> (e.g., reward chart) that has clear, concrete expectations, spelling out specific behaviors/skills to be reinforced.		✔		Increase frequency of providing him stars (on classroom star chart).

Figure 4.4. **Tier I Checklist for Individual Student Planning** *(cont.).*

Social Supports	Identify Strategies That Are Most Relevant			Notes on Implementation
	C	M	A	
1. Use <u>nonverbal language</u> and communication to promote referencing and engagement.				
2. Use strategies and supports that foster a classroom community/team (e.g., "we" language, table names, room themes, photos of shared experiences).				
3. Foster <u>social engagement</u> (e.g., building anticipation, encoding and revisiting shared memories).				
4. Provide students with extra time to process and respond to language in social situations.				
5. Use experience-sharing language (e.g., <u>celebrating</u>, <u>labeling the moment</u>, teamwork).				
6. Use <u>declarative language</u> to foster experience-sharing.				
7. Use <u>self-talk</u> to model Social Thinking® (Winner, 2005), language, and problem-solving.				
8. Use indirect prompts such as declarative statements, gestures, eye gaze, and physical proximity to enhance social awareness.				
9. Use basic Social Thinking® (Winner, 2005) language appropriate for the grade (e.g., <u>flexibility</u>, <u>thinking about me/you</u>® (Winner, 2007), <u>listening with your whole body</u>).				
10. Facilitate teamwork and problem-solving experiences in small groups using developmentally appropriate Social Thinking® (Winner, 2005), language and strategies.				
11. Lead whole class/small groups in <u>role-playing</u> new/difficult situations.				
12. <u>Social narratives</u> and/or <u>cartooning</u> are used to support some students to highlight the social aspects of a situation.				

Figure 4.4. Tier I Checklist for Individual Student Planning *(cont.).*

Academic/Curriculum Supports	Identify Strategies That Are Most Relevant			Notes on Implementation
	C	M	A	
1. Utilize a *variety* of co-teaching styles (e.g., one teach-one assist; parallel group).				
2. Collaboratively plan lessons and prepare all necessary materials to ensure that everything is ready and easily accessible.				
3. Use mini-lesson structure for academic lesson, providing a clear teaching point, modeling, facilitating guided practice, allowing for independent student practice, and then reconvening for a share after independent/group work.				
4. Preview new, challenging material and/or content prior to instruction.	✔			Prior to challenging tasks, teacher should go over steps and expectations.
5. Use flexible small groups to differentiate instruction.				
6. Plan seating strategically to facilitate peer support.				
7. Allow extra time for processing and responding to oral communication.				
8. Provide clear, concise directions for independent work, limiting the number of steps in directions and considering student age, cognitive, and language processing levels.				
9. Use a variety of visuals to clarify lesson, individual, and group work expectations/academic concepts.				
10. Modify presentation of academic activities/tasks to incorporate interests, strengths, or learning styles.				
11. Use graphic organizers for organizing, planning, and reflecting.				
12. Use manipulatives across lessons, whenever relevant, to clarify concepts and increase active engagement.				
13. Use whole-class response strategies in lessons (e.g., slates).				
14. Task analyze complex academic activities to clarify component steps and sequences.				
15. Provide supports to facilitate students' asking for help.				
16. Utilize timers for independent work time cuing.				
17. Pace lessons and amount of independent work required so that it is appropriate for the students' grade and level of academic readiness.				
18. Provide clear expectations for what students should do when they are finished with their independent work.				
19. Provide opportunities for students to work in small groups with the necessary supports.				

Figure 4.4. Tier I Checklist for Individual Student Planning *(cont.).*

In their discussions during and after completing the checklist, the team selected the following strategies and supports for Jonah:

- Use **proximity control/signal interference** during early signs of rumbling, with a teacher positioning herself nearby to check in with Jonah periodically.

- **Increase the use of the break area** by encouraging Jonah to take a break when early signs of escalating frustration first appear.

- Consistently **preview** upcoming challenging tasks and activities; incorporate **visual cues** if needed.

- Provide more **opportunities for making choices** throughout the day.

- Incorporate a **classwide learning experience on making errors as natural** to every person and as a learning opportunity; highlighting errors that the teachers themselves make, recognize, learn from, and correct without self-recrimination.

- Increase the frequency of providing Jonah with **behavior-specific praise** ("catch him being good").

- Provide a **classwide reinforcement system** that rewards students for effort, improvement, and/or completion of activities and tasks rather than for being first or winning.

The team decided to check back in four weeks to see how Jonah was responding to the proposed strategies. Additionally, the team agreed to monitor the occurrence of the more disruptive behaviors, such as meltdowns and intense angry outbursts, that Jonah displayed, using an SABC Chart, shown in Figure 4.5.

Setting Events-Antecedent-Behavior-Consequence (SABC)
Please fill out the following data chart as soon as possible following any disruptive or interfering behavior displayed. The information you provide for each section of the table will help us create a comprehensive picture of the circumstances triggering and maintaining the targeted behavior.

Student's Name: ___Jonah O.___   **Target Behavior:** ___Angry outbursts, tantrum behavior___

Context (Briefly describe the time, activity, nature and place of the activity or task)		Setting Events (Describe **biological, environmental, social factors** that may contribute to the behavior)	Antecedent (What **immediately** precedes the event?)	Target Behavior (Measurable observable terms; **frequency, duration, intensity**)	Consequence (**Response/reaction** to the behavior; what happened afterwards?)
Date: 1/24 **Time:** 10:15	**Activity/ Task:** Independent work on math worksheet	Unexpected change in his morning schedule (returned from speech session late, missed first half of math lesson)	Class was instructed to begin math worksheet	Pacing near his seat; banging his pencil on his desk; making angry comments	Teacher told him to just try to complete whatever he could on the worksheet; she was attending to nearby student; the other teacher was working with a small group across the room.
Date: 1/24 **Time:** 10:19	**Activity/ Task:** Independent work on math worksheet		Teacher alerted the class that they had 3 minutes left to finish their worksheet	He shouted loudly, threw his worksheet onto the floor; made angry comments loudly; repeatedly stomped feet and pounded fists on desk	Teacher went over and instructed him to pick up his paper, encouraged him to take deep breaths and calm down; asked if he wanted to take a break.
Date: 1/24 **Time:** 10:19	**Activity/ Task:** Independent work on math worksheet		Teacher encouraged him to take a break	He protested loudly, continued to stomp his feet; began crying and said "I don't want to take a break now!"	One teacher gathered the class to remove attention from Jonah's behavior, while the other teacher spoke softly to him encouraging him to calm down, get a drink of water.
Date: 2/2 **Time:** 1:27	**Activity/ Task:** Centers (playing board game with 3 peers)	Jonah was absent the previous 2 days due to an illness; he appeared fatigued and was still congested	Teacher alerted the class that they had five minutes left before centers were over and science lesson began	He became physically agitated (bouncing up and down in his seat, tensing his hands, banging his hands on the table and made loud comments telling his classmates to "hurry up!" "I need my turn!" "I have to win!"	His peers told him to stop yelling and hitting the table. The teacher nearby came over and reminded the group of the social narrative they recently read about playing a game. She told Jonah that it was OK if he did not win this time.
Date: 2/2 **Time:** 1:27	**Activity/ Task:** Centers (playing board game with 3 peers)		Jonah took his turn in the game, and after he finished, the teacher alerted the class that center time was over; he was not the winner	He pushed the board game off of the table, yelled, kicked his feet, and cried in protest of not being the winner	1 teacher brought the rest of the class to the science classroom, while another teacher sat with Jonah, encouraging him to take deep breaths, calm down. After approximately 20 minutes, he was calmer, and the teacher prompted him to pick up the board game, put it away, and join the class at science.

Figure 4.5. Setting Events-Antecedent-Behavior-Consequence Chart (SABC).

At the follow-up meeting, the team reviewed the data collected on the SABC Charts, discussed Jonah's progress, and completed a Tier I Implementation Check-In Form (see Figure 4.6).

Tier I Implementation Check-In Form

The first Tier I implementation check-in should take place approximately 3-4 weeks after the student's plan has been implemented. After that, if the student continues to make progress, check-in meetings can take place every 5-6 weeks.

Student: _____Jonah O._____   **Date:** _Tuesday, February 21, 2013_____

Have the recommended strategies and supports (additions/modifications) been implemented?

All of the strategies and supports were implemented, including those that the team agreed to add and/or utilize more frequently.

How did the student respond to the interventions? Have any improvements in the previously identified areas of concern taken place? If so, describe those changes by giving specific examples.

Jonah appears to be more responsive to the teachers when they redirect him; however, he continues to require a great deal of attention from a teacher to help defuse his early rumbling behaviors. He continues to display angry outbursts quite frequently when he gets frustrated, and this often then leads to more intense meltdowns and disruptive behaviors, as documented on SABC Charts during the past four weeks.

Using visual supports appears to be effective for Jonah. He tends to be more successful when the teachers preview expectations and specific steps prior to difficult activities and routines. Incorporating his interests in comic books has also been found to be helpful, as he appears to be more interested in tasks that incorporate his special interest area. Proximity control and providing Jonah with more frequent behavior – specific praise when he is attempting to use his coping skills (e.g., deep breathing, taking a break) also appear to have a positive effect on helping to defuse his rumbling and redirect him back to task.

Next step in supporting this student: Provide the team's recommendation(s).

Tier I strategies should continue to be implemented, but given the frequency of Jonah's interfering behavior and the high degree of attention that is required to help redirect him and defuse his escalating anger when he becomes frustrated, it is recommended that the team complete a Tier II Checklist to identify the areas in which Jonah would be better served by Tier II supports.

Figure 4.6. **Tier I Implementation Check-In Form.**

Although some reduction of interfering behavior was noted, Jonah still frequently engaged in interfering behavior, including outbursts that required a great deal of attention to defuse. Therefore, it was recommended that the team complete a Tier II Checklist of Strategies and Supports for Individual Student Planning (see Figure 4.7) to identify the areas in which an increased level of support would better serve Jonah.

Tier II Strategies and Supports: *Individualized, Planned Interventions*

The following Tier II strategies are used with individual students who require additional, planned interventions and supports. Movement from Tier I to Tier II supports in any domain requires (a) completion of the Tier I Checklist; (b) review and discussion of the Tier I Checklist at a team meeting; and (c) determination that Tier I supports across domains have been implemented adequately and found insufficient to meet the student's needs. Communication with a parent or guardian is recommended.

This individual student form is to be completed by the student's teachers and other members of the school team for planning more effective use of Tier II strategies. Team members should identify the strategies across all four domains that are most relevant to help support the student. For each of the strategies, indicate whether it should be continued, modified, or added to the student's intervention plan by placing a checkmark in the appropriate column, in accordance with the key below. Comments on implementation recommendations may be added in the column on the right, entitled "Notes on Implementation."

Recommendations		
C	**M**	**A**
Continue current use of support	***Modify*** *existing support (Increase or decrease)*	***Add*** *as a new support*

Student Name: Jonah O.   **Date:** Tuesday, February 21, 2013

Sensory Functioning & Self-Regulation Supports	Identify Strategies That Are Most Relevant			Notes on Implementation
	C	**M**	**A**	
1. Implement individual <u>sensory diet/relaxation program</u> created by OT requiring teacher supervision and monitoring by OT.				
2. Use individual <u>sensory tools</u> as directed by OT (e.g. bump seats, wedges, pencil grips, OT vests, slant boards).				
3. **Create and use private work space, separate from peers.**	✔			During challenging tasks, encourage Jonah to use the study carrel to reduce likelihood of becoming distracted by peers finishing a task before he does.
4. Utilize individualized sensory stories.				

Figure 4.7. **Tier II Checklist for Individual Student Planning.**

Behavioral Supports	Identify Strategies That Are Most Relevant			Notes on Implementation
	C	M	A	
1. Provide individualized mini-schedules with teacher support throughout the day.				
2. Use individualized task boards for activities/procedures with teacher monitoring.				
3. **Use individualized visual aid reminders to clarify expectations.**	✔			The more visual cues that can be used, the more concrete and predictable.
4. **Provide individualized, planned priming for new/challenging tasks.**		✔		Work with him 1:1 prior to starting complex tasks to review steps and expectations.
5. Modify and/or simplify challenging tasks.				
6. **Provide individualized, planned opportunities for student choice.**	✔			Continue incorporating opportunities for choice making to enhance his motivation.
7. Use <u>timers</u> on an individualized basis for specific activities/tasks.				
8. **Implement "<u>antiseptic bouncing</u>"/ "just walk, don't talk" strategies.**			✔	Upon noticing Jonah's early signs of rumbling behaviors (frustration), send him on an errand, ask him to take a walk with a teacher to defuse/distract.
9. Implement planned use of <u>high-probability requests</u> to precede challenging activities.				
10. Use individualized & comprehensive planned <u>peer-based supports</u>.				
11. **Create and strategically use <u>Incredible 5-Point Scales</u> tailored to individual student needs.**			✔	Create an individualized "levels of frustration" 5-Point Scale for Jonah to help him identify situations in which he experiences increased frustration and to teach him to use self-regulation strategies.

Figure 4.7. Tier II Checklist for Individual Student Planning (cont.).

Behavioral Supports	Identify Strategies That Are Most Relevant			Notes on Implementation
	C	M	A	
12. Provide functional communication Training (e.g., the <u>HELP program</u> and <u>Break program</u>).			✔	Teach Jonah to request a break when he begins to engage in rumbling behaviors (early signs).
13. Use <u>individualized behavior reinforcement system.</u>			✔	Implement a system of reinforcing attempts to utilize coping skills and replacement behaviors.
14. Create and use individual written <u>social narratives</u> as a preventive measure (see also use of social narratives in Tier II social domain).			✔	Create individualized book of stories aimed at increasing his understanding of challenging situations (e.g., not always being the winner or finishing his work first, making mistakes), and how to respond to them.

Social Supports	Identify Strategies That Are Most Relevant			Notes on Implementation
	C	M	A	
1. Use individualized visuals, <u>Power Cards</u>, problem-solving frameworks (e.g., <u>S.O.C.C.S.S., social autopsies</u>), <u>cartooning</u>, or <u>Social Behavior Mapping</u>© (Winner, 2005) **with individual students to clarify social situations and enhance coping skills.**				Create Power Cards incorporating his special interest in comic book heroes to teach him to identify & use strategies to reduce frustration/ enhance self-regulation.
2. Create <u>social narratives</u> written for and in collaboration with individual students (books can be made up of compiled social narratives written for a particular child) for continued use and reference.				
3. Use 1:1 or small group <u>role-play, video modeling</u>, reflection, and/or priming for new/difficult situations.				

Figure 4.7. **Tier II Checklist for Individual Student Planning (*cont.*).**

Academic/Curriculum Supports	Identify Strategies That Are Most Relevant			Notes on Implementation
	C	M	A	
1. Provide one-to-one and small group previewing for new/challenging content.	✔			Work with him 1:1 prior to starting complex tasks to review steps and expectations.
2. Provide small-group instruction on a consistent basis for challenging content.				
3. Incorporate individual student interests to increase motivation.	✔			Continue incorporating his special interest areas (comic book heroes) to enhance his motivation.
4. Use individualized visuals for lesson expectations and independent or group work expectations.				
5. Utilize individualized graphic organizers, simplified as needed.				
6. Provide differentiated and simplified content, as needed.				
7. Modify work expectations for product and, when needed (e.g., decreased amount of work required).				
8. Decrease expectation for time-on-task and/or duration of learning activities.				
9. Provide individualized note-taking supports for lessons.				
10. Provide teacher support during transitions by checking in with student to ensure understanding of next steps.				
11. Create checklists for student with complex tasks broken into steps/parts.				
12. Provide and monitor independent use of individual organizational systems by student (e.g., binders, color coded systems, bins).				
13. Establish a self-monitoring system to enhance active participation.				
14. Use timers for individual students to improve time management during work periods.				
15. Plan and implement specific peer supports.				

Figure 4.7. **Tier II Checklist for Individual Student Planning (*cont.*).**

Upon completing the Tier II Checklist, the team decided to add the following strategies and supports to Jonah's plan:

- Provide **increased one-to-one support** during new and/or particularly challenging tasks.

- **Create a private workspace ("office")** in a quieter area of the classroom for Jonah to use when working on difficult tasks requiring sustained concentration (may also lessen the likelihood of him noticing other students finishing their work before him, causing him to become anxious and upset).

- Use strategies such as **"antiseptic bouncing" and "just walk don't talk"** to defuse early signs of rumbling or frustration, indicating that a meltdown was likely.

- Provide **individualized visual supports** for Jonah, such as a visual reminder card about what to do when he is having difficulty or getting upset.

- Create an individualized **Incredible 5-Point Scale** to help Jonah learn to recognize instances in which he experiences increased levels of stress, as a first step in the process of enhancing his self-monitoring skill.

- **Incorporate Jonah's interests** (comic books) into tasks/assignments (when possible) to enhance motivation.

- Create and utilize individual **social narratives** aimed at increasing Jonah's understanding of challenging situations (making mistakes, not finishing his work first, not always being the winner of a game) and how to respond to them.

- Use **Power Cards** incorporating Jonah's special interest in comic books to teach Jonah to identify and utilize strategies for enhancing self-regulation.

- Use **functional communication training (the Break program)** to teach Jonah to request a break when he begins to get upset and engage in rumbling behaviors.

- Implement an **individualized reinforcement system** in which Jonah is reinforced for utilizing (or attempting to utilize) his coping skills and replacement behaviors.

Tier II strategies and supports were implemented for approximately four weeks, after which the team met again to review Jonah's progress. The team continued to monitor Jonah's functioning using an SABC Chart (see Figure 4.8) to document any meltdowns or intense angry outbursts he displayed.

Setting Events-Antecedent-Behavior-Consequence (SABC)
Please fill out the following data chart as soon as possible following any disruptive or interfering behavior displayed. The information you provide for each section of the table will help us create a comprehensive picture of the circumstances triggering and maintaining the targeted behavior.

Student's Name: ___Jonah O.___   **Target Behavior:** ___Angry outbursts, tantrum behavior___

Context (Briefly describe the time, activity, nature and place of the activity or task)		Setting Events (Describe **biological, environmental, social factors** that may contribute to the behavior)	Antecedent (What **immediately** precedes the event?)	Target Behavior (Measurable observable terms; **frequency, duration, intensity**)	Consequence (**Response/reaction** to the behavior; what happened afterwards?)
Date: 2/27 **Time:** 1:05	**Activity/ Task:** Independent work – finishing up writing assignment	He was sick over the weekend and stayed home from school on Friday; he still reports feeling tired, and congested.	Class was instructed to return to their seats and begin working on their writing assignments	He took out his work, began writing, but quickly became increasingly upset. He erased his page a number of times, started getting frustrated, made angry comments, started pacing	Teacher told him to just try to complete whatever he could on the worksheet; she was attending to nearby student; the other teacher was working with a small group across the room.
Date: 2/27 **Time:** 1:10	**Activity/ Task:** Independent work – finishing up writing assignment		His teacher told him to just try to complete whatever he could before the period ended	He took his Power Card out, read it, and used one of the suggestions written on it (to calm down). He then worked with the teacher without further escalation in behavior; was able to complete most of the work by the end of the period	The teacher provided behavior-specific praise for using his coping tools to help calm down.
Date: 3/9 **Time:** 11:47	**Activity/ Task:** Learning Centers (math center – playing a game with 3 peers)		It was nearing the end of the game; teacher reminded the class they had 3 minutes left	Jonah appeared to be increasingly anxious, as he was not going to finish the game his group was playing. He started pacing and making angry comments	The teacher moved closer to Jonah when noticing he was getting upset and reminded him to use a coping tool to help calm down. She used distraction (got him thinking about a special interest item – comic books). He did not escalate any further. She provided behavior-specific praise!

Figure 4.8. **Setting Events-Antecedent-Behavior-Consequence Chart (SABC).**

Based on the SABC data collected and teacher comments on the Tier II Implementation Check-in Form (see Figure 4.9), the team concluded that Jonah was responding well to the increased level of support being provided. Specifically, they noted that the frequency and intensity of his meltdowns and angry outbursts had been substantially reduced following the implementation of the Tier II strategies and supports. Jonah benefited from the incorporation of his special interests and other modifications made to challenging academic tasks, as well as his use of a work carrel, the break program, and the other strategies aimed at enhancing his self-regulation skills.

Tier II Implementation Check-In Form

The first Tier II implementation check-in should take place approximately 3-4 weeks after the student's plan has been implemented. After that, if the student continues to make progress, check-in meetings can take place every 5-6 weeks.

Student: _____Jonah O._____ **Date:** _Tuesday, March 20, 2013_ _____

Have the recommended strategies and supports (additions/modifications) been implemented?

All of the strategies and supports were implemented, including those that the team agreed to add and/or more frequently utilize.

How did the student respond to the interventions? Have any improvements in the previously identified areas of concern taken place? If so, describe those changes by giving specific examples.

Jonah appears to be more responsive to the teachers when they redirect him; he continues to respond positively to the use of visual supports, particularly during more challenging tasks and during times when teachers notice that he is becoming frustrated (demonstrating early signs of rumbling behavior). When the teachers are able to implement the strategies prior to escalation of interfering behavior, Jonah more readily utilizes his coping skills (taking deep breaths, using his Power Cards) and, as a result, fewer meltdowns and angry outbursts have been noticed. SABC data collected during the past four weeks document the reduction of interfering behavior. The frequency in his tantrums and angry outbursts has been substantially reduced since putting the Tier II strategies in place, and the teachers noticed that the intensity of the few outbursts that he does display has significantly been reduced. He is more responsive to redirection and increased teacher support upon noticing early rumbling behaviors.

Providing Jonah with increased teacher support, particularly prior to more challenging tasks and upon noticing early signs of frustration, appears to be beneficial in reducing the intensity and frequency of his interfering behavior. Using social narratives, Power Cards, and the Incredible 5-Point Scale appears to be helpful in enhancing self-regulation and reducing his frustration level.

Next step in supporting this student: Provide the team's recommendation(s).

Given Jonah's positive response to the various Tier I and Tier II strategies, it is recommended that the team continue to implement them and reevaluate his progress in four to five weeks to determine if any modifications need to be made.

Figure 4.9. Tier II Implementation Check-In Form.

Given the progress Jonah was making with Tier II supports, the team decided to continue implementing the plan that was in place, while checking in every five to six weeks to determine if any modifications were needed. The Tier II plan remained in place for the remainder of the school year as Jonah continued to make progress. His interfering behaviors declined significantly, and he frequently utilized more adaptive replacement behaviors and coping skills in the face of social and academic challenges, making it possible to gradually reduce the use of one-to-one attention by teachers.

The Tier III Checklist of Strategies and Supports for Individual Students

Andrew: Tier III Case Study

Andrew, a student in a third-grade ASD Nest classroom, was experiencing difficulty across multiple areas. His teachers became increasingly concerned and scheduled a discussion of Andrew's functioning during the October case conference meeting of the ASD Nest team. They identified four primary areas that were of greatest concern, accompanied by illustrations (displayed in Table 4.1).

Table 4.1
Andrew's Areas of Concern

Area of Concern	Illustration
Difficulty focusing on tasks	It took him a great deal of time to start working on the first step of most activities or routines. He needed multiple prompts to complete the routine of unpacking his backpack upon entering the classroom in the morning although he had followed a similar routine every morning since kindergarten. It took Andrew so much time to complete that routine that he often missed most of the first class activity of the day.
Frequently distracted by thoughts related to his special interests (video games and songs)	He tended to make comments out loud on events he recalled that were unrelated to the activity at hand. He often repeated dialogue from a favorite movie or sang the lyrics to a favorite song.
Difficulty with writing activities	He had graphomotor challenges, for which he had been receiving individual OT sessions in school since kindergarten, and organizational challenges in writing. He was seldom able to complete written assignments; during writing activities his verbalizations became louder and his other off-task behavior increased significantly.
Difficulty with transitions (between locations and between activities)	He often appeared "lost," wandering around the room without asking for help or using the actions of peers to guide him. He then tended to produce an increasingly loud and animated running commentary on thoughts unrelated to the task and appeared unaware of whether it was an appropriate time for him to speak or whether others were listening, which greatly impeded his relationships with peers who became increasingly upset by his interruptions of classroom activities.

After the teachers had finished presenting their observations of Andrew, other members of the team, such as Andrew's current OT, provided additional information, and the team completed a Tier I Checklist of Strategies and Supports for Individual Students on Andrew. The completed checklist is presented in Figure 4.10.

**Tier I
ASD Nest Program
Three-Tier Model**

Tier I Checklist for Individual Student Planning: *Relevant for All Nest Classes*

The following strategies are strongly recommended for use with all ASD Nest classes. This individual student form is to be completed by the student's teachers and other members of the school team for planning more effective use of Tier I strategies. Team members should identify the strategies across all four domains that are most relevant to help support the student. For each of the strategies, indicate whether it should be continued, modified, or added to the student's intervention plan by placing a checkmark in the appropriate column, in accordance with the key below. Comments on implementation recommendations may be added in the column on the right, entitled "Notes on Implementation."

Recommendations		
C	**M**	**A**
Continue *current use of support*	**Modify** *existing support (Increase or decrease)*	**Add** *as a new support*

Student Name: Andrew N.　　　　　　　　　　　　**Date:** Wednesday, October 19, 2013

Sensory Functioning & Self-Regulation Supports	Identify Strategies That Are Most Relevant			Notes on Implementation
	C	M	A	
1. Modify classroom environments to accommodate sensory sensitivities and prevent sensory overload.				
2. Balance arousing and calming activities across the day.				
3. **Create and promote the use of a <u>break area</u> that contains calming materials for self-regulation.**	✔			Offer him a break prior to challenging activities (e.g., writing tasks).
4. Monitor teacher voice volume so that it is appropriate to individuals in the class and to the size of the group.				
5. **Utilize whole-class movement activities throughout the day.**		✔		Brief, yet vigorous exercises prior to prolonged periods requiring sustained attention.
6. Use classroom relaxation activities throughout the day.				
7. **Make <u>sensory tools</u> available, as appropriate (e.g., work carrels, headphones, fidgets).**			✔	Work carrel to complete writing tasks; head-phones to use in noisy settings.

Figure 4.10. Tier I Checklist for Individual Student Planning.

Behavioral Supports	Identify Strategies That Are Most Relevant			Notes on Implementation
	C	M	A	
1. Display daily <u>class schedule</u> and reference frequently.				
2. Organize classroom to minimize visual distraction.				
3. Utilize <u>visual aids</u> and concrete examples to supplement verbal directions.				
4. Provide opportunities for students to make choices throughout the day.				
5. Incorporate student strengths & interests into learning activities.		✓		Increase frequency – incorporate his interests into lessons, assignment & homework.
6. Tell students what to do rather than what not to do.				
7. Use clear, concise, concrete language to clarify expectations.		✓		Increase frequency of providing specific instructions.
8. "<u>Catch them being good</u>" and provide behavior-specific praise.				
9. Use <u>proximity control</u>/<u>signal interference</u> preventively.			✓	Teachers should move near him to signal/ redirect him when he begins verbalizing.
10. Highlight appropriate behavior in peers.				
11. Anticipate upcoming preferred activities ("<u>looking forward to</u>" approach).				
12. Preview upcoming activities/transitions/expectations.				
13. Use and refer to the <u>Incredible 5-Point Scale</u> to concretize abstract concepts.				
14. Use visual <u>task sequencing boards</u> for routines and activities.			✓	Checklists of steps for challenging task are needed.
15. Select nurturing <u>peer buddies</u> to provide support.				
16. Use classwide <u>visual timers</u> for transitions and activities to indicate activity duration.				
17. Implement <u>classwide reinforcement system</u> (e.g., reward chart) that has clear, concrete expectations, spelling out specific behaviors/skills to be reinforced.				

Figure 4.10. **Tier I Checklist for Individual Student Planning** *(cont.).*

Social Supports	Identify Strategies That Are Most Relevant			Notes on Implementation
	C	M	A	
1. Use <u>nonverbal language</u> and communication to promote referencing and engagement.				
2. Use strategies and supports that foster a classroom community/ team (e.g., "we" language, table names, room themes, photos of shared experiences).				
3. Foster <u>social engagement</u> (e.g., building anticipation, encoding and revisiting shared memories).				
4. Provide students with extra time to process and respond to language in social situations.				
5. Use experience-sharing language (e.g., <u>celebrating</u>, <u>labeling the moment</u>, teamwork).				
6. Use <u>declarative language</u> to foster experience-sharing.				
7. Use <u>self-talk</u> to model Social Thinking® (Winner, 2005), language, and problem-solving.				
8. Use indirect prompts such as declarative statements, gestures, eye gaze, and physical proximity to enhance social awareness.				
9. Use basic Social Thinking® (Winner, 2005) language appropriate for the grade (e.g., <u>flexibility</u>, <u>thinking about me/you</u>® (Winner, 2007), <u>listening with your whole body</u>).				
10. Facilitate teamwork and problem-solving experiences in small groups using developmentally appropriate Social Thinking® (Winner, 2005) language and strategies.				
11. Lead whole class/small groups in <u>role-playing</u> new/difficult situations.				
12. <u>Social narratives</u> and/or <u>cartooning</u> are used to support some students to highlight the social aspects of a situation.				

Academic/Curriculum Supports	Identify Strategies That Are Most Relevant			Notes on Implementation
	C	M	A	
1. Utilize a variety of <u>co-teaching styles</u> (e.g., one teach-one assist; parallel group).				
2. Collaboratively plan lessons and prepare all necessary materials to ensure that everything is ready and easily accessible.				
3. Use mini-lesson structure for academic lesson, providing a clear teaching point, modeling, facilitating guided practice, allowing for independent student practice, and then reconvening for a share after independent/group work.				

Figure 4.10. **Tier I Checklist for Individual Student Planning** *(cont.).*

Academic/Curriculum Supports	Identify Strategies That Are Most Relevant			Notes on Implementation
	C	M	A	
4. **Preview new, challenging material and/or content prior to instruction.**	✔			Prior to challenging tasks (writing), teacher previews steps & expectations to ensure he understands.
5. Use flexible small groups to differentiate instruction.				
6. Plan seating strategically to facilitate peer support.				
7. **Allow extra time for processing and responding to oral communication.**		✔		Increase frequency; provide enough time to comprehend directions, check for understanding.
8. **Provide clear, concise directions for independent work, limiting the number of steps in directions and considering student age, cognitive, and language processing levels.**		✔		Increase frequency; modify number of steps (simplify).
9. **Use a variety of visuals to clarify lesson, individual, and group work expectations/academic concepts.**	✔			
10. Modify presentation of academic activities/tasks to incorporate interests, strengths, or learning styles.				
11. **Use graphic organizers for organizing, planning, and reflecting.**			✔	Add these to help him organize his thoughts and make writing tasks easier.
12. Use manipulatives across lessons, whenever relevant, to clarify concepts and increase active engagement.				
13. Use whole-class response strategies in lessons (e.g., slates).				
14. **Task analyze complex academic activities to clarify component steps and sequences.**		✔		Increase frequency; break down complex tasks into more simplified steps to clarify expectations.
15. Provide supports to facilitate students' asking for help.				
16. Utilize timers for independent work time cuing.				
17. Pace lessons and amount of independent work required so that it is appropriate for the students' grade and level of academic readiness.				
18. Provide clear expectations for what students should do when they are finished with their independent work.				
19. Provide opportunities for students to work in small groups with the necessary supports.				

Figure 4.10. **Tier I Checklist for Individual Student Planning *(cont.)*.**

The following strategies were designated for implementation:

- Incorporate more **classwide movement activities** throughout the day, particularly during long class lessons on the carpet.

- Invite Andrew to use sensory tools such as the classroom **work carrel and headphones** (in noisy, distracting settings) to enhance his concentration on assignments that require him to produce written work.

- Encourage Andrew to use the **break area** for a brief period prior to the start of activities that he finds particularly challenging.

- When providing instructions to the class, highlight expectations by **telling the students in as clear, concise, and concrete language as possible what to do,** avoiding giving multiple steps at one time; **provide ample time for students to process instructions.**

- **Incorporate visual cues** into routines throughout the day. Add **visually represented behavioral expectations, and graphic organizers** during lessons on writing to help students better organize, plan, and execute their work.

- Utilize **proximity control/signal interference** in a preventive manner. A teacher should move near Andrew when he begins verbalizing (talking to himself aloud) to signal/redirect him back to task and remind him of behavioral expectations (e.g., work quietly).

- **Incorporate Andrew's interests** into various lessons and homework sheets to increase his motivation to complete them.

- Use **priming** to prepare students for upcoming transitions and to clarify expectations prior to starting the next activity.

The team agreed to monitor Andrew's functioning for three weeks after the recommended Tier I strategies had been implemented and then meet again to assess his progress and outline the next steps to best support him. When the team reconvened to discuss Andrew's response to the supports that had been implemented, it was noted that while he had made some slight improvements, he still continued to present pervasive and significant challenges. The team concluded that Andrew needed more individualized and intensive strategies. Therefore, they completed a Tier II Checklist, which is shown in Figure 4.11.

Tier II Strategies and Supports: *Individualized, planned interventions*

The following Tier II strategies are used with individual students who require additional, planned interventions and supports. Movement from Tier I to Tier II supports in any domain requires (a) completion of the Tier I Checklist; (b) review and discussion of the Tier I Checklist at a team meeting; and (c) determination that Tier I supports across domains have been implemented adequately and found insufficient to meet the student's needs. Communication with a parent or guardian is recommended.

This individual student form is to be completed by the student's teachers and other members of the school team for planning more effective use of Tier II strategies. Team members should identify the strategies across all four domains that are most relevant to help support the student. For each of the strategies, indicate whether it should be continued, modified, or added to the student's intervention plan by placing a checkmark in the appropriate column, in accordance with the key below. Comments on implementation recommendations may be added in the column on the right, entitled "Notes on Implementation."

Recommendations		
C	M	A
Continue current use of support	*Modify* existing support *(Increase or decrease)*	*Add* as a new support

Student Name: Andrew N.   **Date:** Wednesday, November 30, 2013

Sensory Functioning & Self-Regulation Supports	Identify Strategies That Are Most Relevant			Notes on Implementation
	C	M	A	
1. Implement individual <u>sensory diet/relaxation program</u> created by OT requiring teacher supervision and monitoring by OT.				
2. Use individual <u>sensory tools</u> as directed by OT (e.g. bump seats, wedges, pencil grips, OT vests, slant boards).			✔	OT recommends using pencil grips and slant boards during writing assignments.
3. Create and use private work space, separate from peers.	✔			During challenging tasks, encourage Andrew to use the study carrel to reduce likelihood of becoming distracted by peers finishing a task before he does.
4. Utilize individualized sensory stories.				

Figure 4.11. **Tier II Checklist for Individual Student Planning.**

Behavioral Supports	Identify Strategies That Are Most Relevant			Notes on Implementation
	C	M	A	
1. Provide individualized mini-schedules with teacher support throughout the day.		✔		Increase the use of individualized schedule displaying upcoming 2-3 activities to increase predictability.
2. Use individualized task boards for activities/procedures with teacher monitoring.	✔			Continue using visual representations of steps for complex tasks.
3. Use individualized visual aid reminders to clarify expectations.	✔			Continue using visual cues to make expectations more concrete and predictable.
4. Provide individualized, planned priming for new/challenging tasks.		✔		Increase frequency of working with him 1:1 prior to starting complex tasks to review steps & expectations.
5. Modify and/or simplify challenging tasks.	✔			Continue to simplify the content of more challenging areas (e.g., writing related tasks).
6. Provide individualized, planned opportunities for student choice.				
7. Use <u>timers</u> on an individualized basis for specific activities/tasks.			✔	Use individual timers to help increase the predictability of time remaining on more difficult tasks.
8. Implement "<u>antiseptic bouncing</u>"/ "just walk, don't talk" strategies.				
9. Implement planned use of <u>high-probability requests</u> to precede challenging activities.				
10. Use individualized & comprehensive planned <u>peer-based supports</u>.				
11. Create and strategically use <u>Incredible 5-Point Scales</u> tailored to individual student needs.				
12. Provide functional communication training (e.g., the <u>Help program</u> and <u>Break program</u>).			✔	Teach Andrew to request assistance when he does not understand what to do or is having difficulty with a task.
13. Use <u>individualized behavior reinforcement system.</u>			✔	Implement a system of reinforcing attempts to utilize coping skills and replacement behaviors.

Figure 4.11. **Tier II Checklist for Individual Student Planning** *(cont.).*

Behavioral Supports	Identify Strategies That Are Most Relevant			Notes on Implementation
	C	M	A	
14. Create and use individual <u>social narrative</u> books as a preventive measure (see also use of social narratives in Tier II social domain).			✔	Create individualized book of stories aimed at increasing his understanding of challenging situations (working with peers, taking turns when talking with classmates).

Social Supports	Identify Strategies That Are Most Relevant			Notes on Implementation
	C	M	A	
1. Use individualized visuals, <u>Power Cards</u>, problem solving frameworks (e.g., <u>S.O.C.C.S.S., social autopsies</u>), <u>cartooning</u>, or <u>Social Behavior Mapping</u>© (Winner, 2005) with individual students to clarify social situations and enhance coping skills.				
2. Create <u>social narratives</u> written for and in collaboration with individual students (books can be made up of compiled social narratives written for a particular child) for continued use and reference.				
3. Use 1:1 or small group <u>role play, video modeling</u>, reflection, and/or priming for new/difficult situations.				

Academic/Curriculum Supports	Identify Strategies That Are Most Relevant			Notes on Implementation
	C	M	A	
1. **Provide one-to-one and small group previewing for new/ challenging content.**	✔			Increase frequency of working with him 1:1 prior to starting complex tasks to review steps and expectations.
2. Provide small-group instruction on a consistent basis for challenging content.				
3. **Incorporate individual student interests to increase motivation.**	✔			Continue incorporating his special interest areas (music, video game characters) to enhance his motivation.

Figure 4.11. **Tier II Checklist for Individual Student Planning *(cont.).***

Academic/Curriculum Supports	Identify Strategies That Are Most Relevant			Notes on Implementation
	C	M	A	
4. Use individualized visuals for lesson expectations and independent or group work expectations.		✔		Incorporate more visuals into presentation of abstract concepts and difficult tasks.
5. Utilize individualized graphic organizers, simplified as needed.		✔		Increased use of graphic organizers can help provide him with structure & a way to organize his thoughts, simplifying writing tasks.
6. Provide differentiated and simplified content, as needed.	✔			Continue to simplify the content of more challenging areas (writing) by presenting concepts more concretely.
7. Modify work expectations for product and, when needed (e.g., decreased amount of work required).	✔			Continue to reduce the amount of work he is expected to produce (for writing tasks).
8. Decrease expectation for time-on-task and/or duration of learning activities.	✔			Continue to reduce the length of time he is expected to stay on task so that he experiences greater opportunities of success.
9. Provide individualized note-taking supports for lessons.		✔		Increase the use of note-taking (intersperse tasks requiring him to write with those where the teacher dictates for him).
10. Provide teacher support during transitions by checking in with student to ensure understanding of next steps.	✔			Teacher should continue to work with him prior to and during transitions – ensure he understands expectations and what to do.
11. Create checklists for student with complex tasks broken into steps/parts.		✔		Increase frequency of use of checklists to break down complex tasks into simple steps.
12. Provide and monitor independent use of individual organizational systems by student (e.g., binders, color coded systems, bins).				
13. Establish a self-monitoring system to enhance active participation.				
14. Use timers for individual students to improve time management during work periods.	✔			Continue providing visual representation of time remaining on challenging tasks.
15. Plan and implement specific peer supports.				

Figure 4.11. **Tier II Checklist for Individual Student Planning** *(cont.).*

Upon completing the Tier II Checklist, the team outlined an intervention plan that incorporated the following Tier II strategies:

- The OT recommended using **pencil grips and a slant board** to address his graphomotor difficulties, and she designed a **plan of various calming and alerting exercises** for Andrew to use throughout the day to help him to modulate his level of arousal.

- Present independent writing tasks at the **work carrel**, with one of the teachers providing proximity support and **additional one-to-one support** to help him get started on difficult assignments, tasks, and transitions.

- Utilize **individualized visual supports** throughout the day: Add **mini-schedules** that display upcoming activities and transitions. Incorporate **individualized task sequencing boards and checklists for difficult routines** into classroom activities; one of the teachers should work individually with Andrew to help him use the checklists to organize and structure his independent work activities.

- **Challenging activities, such as writing tasks, were modified** both at school and for homework assignments. The **amount of work that was expected was reduced**, and the **expectation for his written product was modified.** Instead of having 10 or so math problems for homework, Andrew was presented with a homework sheet consisting of 5 problems that he was required to do, and on the other side of the paper another 5 problems that were optional.

- **Social narratives** were created for Andrew to address specific situations that remained challenging for him (e.g., understanding the perspectives of others). A book of these social narratives was created for him, which he was able to access whenever he took a break or wanted to review them.

- Create and implement an **individualized behavior reinforcement system**, whereby Andrew earns stickers for displaying appropriate behavior (i.e., remaining on task and stopping loud verbalizations when redirected by the teacher). Upon receiving a specified number of stickers within a given time period, Andrew is to be provided with the opportunity to choose from a menu of rewards (e.g., use the computer, listen to music, talk with a preferred adult or classmate about an area of interest).

The team continued to monitor Andrew's response to the implementation of the Tier II strategies, and they collected and analyzed SABC data during this time, as shown in Figure 4.12.

Setting Events-Antecedent-Behavior-Consequence (SABC)
Please fill out the following data chart as soon as possible following any disruptive or interfering behavior displayed. The information you provide for each section of the table will help us create a comprehensive picture of the circumstances triggering and maintaining the targeted behavior.

Student's Name: Andrew N.   **Target Behavior:** Off task/staring/distracted; verbalizations (talking to himself aloud)

Context (Briefly describe the time, activity, nature and place of the activity or task)		Setting Events (Describe **biological, environmental, social factors** that may contribute to the behavior)	Antecedent (What **immediately** precedes the event?)	Target Behavior (Measurable observable terms; **frequency, duration, intensity**)	Consequence (**Response/reaction** to the behavior; what happened afterwards?)
Date: 12/1 Time: 8:15	Activity/Task: Transition into classroom (unpacking routine)		The class walked from cafeteria, & students were instructed to go into classroom and unpack their bags to get ready for morning meeting	He wandered around the room with his coat & backpack on for approximately 6 mins, talking to himself; did not follow instructions, ask for help, or reference peers who were unpacking their bags	Ms. S reminded him to unpack his bag.
Date: 12/1 Time: 8:21	Activity/Task: Transition into classroom (unpacking routine)		He was reminded to unpack his bag and get ready for morning meeting	He hung up his coat (once Ms. S provided a prompt to show him where to put it), went to his desk, opened his bag, and then sat and stared out the window for approximately 4 mins	Ms. S redirected him back to task (reminded him to continue unpacking). She provided prompts to help complete the rest of the task (total time to unpack: 23 mins).
Date: 12/1 Time: 10:05	Activity/Task: Writer's Workshop	Schedule changed unexpectedly – Speech session was moved to the afternoon	Class was instructed to begin writing assignment (independent work at their tables)	He sat and stared at a poster on the wall for about 3 mins (he did not take out his folder and start writing as his classmates did). He talked to himself aloud	Ms. A stood next to him and redirected him (reminded him to take out his folder and work on his writing assignment). She went to help another student & kept checking in on him.
Date: 12/1 Time: 10:15	Activity/Task: Writer's Workshop		Ms. A continued providing prompts reminding him to refocus and work on his writing assignment	He sat with his pencil & paper staring at his paper, wrote a few words after being prompted, then stopped, stared, and started verbalizing aloud until being prompted again	Ms. A sat next to him, and helped him generate ideas to write about. She provided continual prompts & redirected him to continue the task. He wrote 2-3 sentences during the 30-minute period.
Date: 12/5 Time: 8:05	Activity/Task: Unpacking routine		He was prompted to continue unpacking and use his visual task board	He went through the remaining steps, needing prompts from Ms. A to check his task board	Ms. A continued prompting him to use his task board, and redirected his verbalizations during the rest of the routine. Total time to unpack: 15mins.
Date: 12/5 Time: 8:08	Activity/Task: Unpacking routine		He was prompted to continue unpacking and use his visual task board	He went through the remaining steps, needing prompts from Ms. A to check his task board	Ms. A continued prompting him to use his task board, and redirected his verbalizations during the rest of the routine. Total time to unpack: 15 mins.

Figure 4.12. **Setting Events-Antecedent-Behavior-Consequence Chart (SABC).**

Date/Time	Activity/Task				
Date: 12/14 Time: 1:15	**Activity/ Task:** Writer's Workshop	Absent the day before with a cold; he still seemed congested and had a runny nose	Whole class on carpet for mini-lesson; Ms. S asked a question, instructed students to raise their hand to share their response & wait to be called on	He did not raise his hand and began answering the question without referencing his peers or the teachers.	Ms. S held up a visual cue card (picture symbol of "raise your hand") and reminded him to wait his turn. She was seated next to him and continued to provide visual cues and verbal reminders as he intermittently interrupted classmates who were answering questions.
Date: 12/14 Time: 1:33	**Activity/ Task:** Writer's Workshop		Class sent from carpet back to tables to do independent work – Ms. S instructed them to edit their writing assignment from the previous day	He slowly returned to his table after several prompts from Ms. S; sat and stared for several minutes, started verbalizing until redirected back to task	Ms. S sat next to him, provided a written checklist of 3 steps for him to complete. He needed multiple reminders to reference the checklist and complete the steps. He got through 2 steps by the end of the period.
Date: 12/18 Time: 11:55	**Activity/ Task:** Packing up routine (before going to lunch & afternoon specials)		Ms. A instructed the class to pack up backpacks and get ready for lunch. They would be going to art and science in afternoon, and needed to get bags ready for dismissal before they left their classroom for the afternoon	He used his visual task sequencing board for packing up routine and started on the first step. He needed to be redirected by Ms. A several times to stop verbalizing & continue using his task board and refocus on packing up	Ms. A stood next to him and redirected him throughout the routine. She reminded him to use his task sequencing board (which he did), and he completed all steps in approximately 10 minutes; he joined his classmates in the lunchroom.
Date: 12/19 Time: 9:20	**Activity/ Task:** Transition from Speech Club to Reader's Workshop	Speech club ran 5 minutes longer than usual, so he came into Reader's Workshop mini-lesson late	He was instructed to quietly walk into classroom and join his classmates on the carpet for Reader's Workshop	He walked in talking to himself aloud (verbalizations unrelated to the task). Wandered around classroom until redirected to sit next to Ms. A	Ms. A took him aside and explained what he had missed, reminded him of expectations for sitting in the group quietly (used visual cue cards). They joined the class.
Date: 12/19 Time: 9:27	**Activity/ Task:** Reader's Workshop (mini-lesson)		Ms. S was conducting a read-aloud the on carpet with the whole class; she asked students questions (reminded them to raise their hands & wait to be called on)	Several times during the read-aloud, he started to verbalize (off-topic comments); Ms. A redirected him with visual cue card. He interrupted a peer answering a question & was redirected by Ms. A. He raised his hand to answer a question	Ms. S called on him, provided behavior-specific praise for raising his hand & waiting his turn. Ms. A took out his reward chart and gave him a sticker.

Figure 4.12. **Setting Events-Antecedent-Behavior-Consequence Chart (SABC)** *(cont.).*

After a period of approximately four weeks, the team met for a case conference to review the SABC data and discuss Andrew's progress. They completed a Tier II Implementation Check-in Form, which appears in Figure 4.13.

Tier II Implementation Check-In Form

The first Tier II implementation check-in should take place approximately 3-4 weeks after the student's plan has been implemented. After that, if the student continues to make progress, check-in meetings can take place every 5-6 weeks.

Student: _____ Andrew N. _____   **Date:** _____ Wednesday, December 21, 2013 _____

Have the recommended strategies and supports (additions/modifications) been implemented?

All of the strategies and supports were implemented, including those that the team agreed to add and/or modify (use more frequently).

How did the student respond to the interventions? Have any improvements in the previously identified areas of concern taken place? If so, describe those changes by giving specific examples.

Andrew continues to be responsive to the increased level of attention and support he is provided, and when he is redirected by his teacher, he is able to more easily shift his focus back to task. However, he continues to require a great deal of attention from the teacher to prime him before each activity, to keep him on task, and to redirect his verbalizations.

Using visual supports appears to be effective for Andrew. Providing him with concrete steps and expectations on task sequencing boards and previewing them prior to the start of routines and activities seems to help him get started on tasks more quickly than in the past. Creating and implementing individualized social narratives written specifically for Andrew has been helpful in providing him with greater awareness and understanding of the impact of disruptive behaviors.

Next step in supporting this student: Provide the team's recommendation(s).

Tier II strategies should continue to be implemented, but given the frequency of Andrew's interfering behavior and the high level of attention that is still required to help him, it is recommended that the team move into Tier III in the Behavior and Academic domains. The team plans to meet with Andrew's parents and complete the Functional Behavior Assessment Interview, Academic Screening Form, as well as the Tier III Checklist to identify the areas in which Andrew would be better served by an even more intensive level of supports and strategies.

Figure 4.13. **Tier II Implementation Check-In Form.**

Although the team noted that Andrew was responding positively to many of the Tier II strategies, he was still experiencing considerable difficulty with writing assignments and was not producing much written work. Additionally, his difficulties with sustaining attention and completing most routines and activities continued to require a great deal of individual support throughout the day. Thus, the team decided that Andrew needed Tier III strategies in both the behavior and the academic domains.

Prior to implementing any Tier III interventions, Andrew's parents met with his teachers and other selected members of the team. At that meeting, the Academic Screening Form (Figure 4. 14) was completed, and the parents responded to questions from the Functional Behavior Assessment Interview Form.

Tier III Academic Screening Form

Entry into any Tier III intervention *must* involve a parent/guardian meeting to gather and share information about supports and strategies to be used. The team must also meet to complete this form for the student's file prior to implementing any Tier III strategies. All Tier III interventions are intensive, individual supports for students who continue to struggle with most grade-level expectations and receive a rating of "1" (the lowest rating on a four-point scale) in reading, writing, or math on their report card. Supplemental programs for decoding, math, or writing may need to be considered to provide further support for the student.

Date: __Andrew N.__   Student Name: __Wednesday, January 11, 2013__

Persons present at meeting: __Co-teachers, speech therapist, OT, social worker, parents.__

Before considering Tier III Academic Interventions, the team must take the following into account and document actions taken to examine these possible contributing factors

POSSIBLE CONTRIBUTING FACTOR	If yes, person/s responsible & implementation	Initial when completed
Has there been a sudden change in the child's academic performance over the past several months? ☐ Yes ☒ No *Notes:* Andrew's academic performance has remained unchanged; he continues to struggle to produce written work and to complete most academic assignments.	Who: _____ What:_____ By when: _____	
Has the student's file (e.g., cumulative record) and/or recent assessments or observation reports been reviewed to identify possible sudden change in the child's academic performance over the past several months? ☒ Yes ☐ No *Notes:* The team reviewed his file and did not find any sudden changes in his performance.	Who: _Teachers *& SLP____ What: _Reviewed his files____ By when: _January_____	
Is there any indication that:		
A comprehensive medical and/or neurological evaluation might be needed? ☒ Yes ☐ No *Notes:* It was recommended that his parents bring him to a neurologist for comprehensive evaluation.	Who: ___Parents_____ What: Neurological evaluation___ By when: __January_____	
A comprehensive vision evaluation might be needed (e.g., to rule out visual tracking difficulties, nearsightedness, farsightedness, convergence issues)? ☐ Yes ☒ No *Notes:* Andrew already receives individualized OT sessions weekly.	Who: _____ What:_____ By when: _____	
An occupational therapy evaluation might be needed? ❑ Yes ☒ No *Notes:* Andrew will be evaluated for an assistive technology device to address his difficulties with writing.	Who: _____ What:_____ By when: _____	
An assistive technology evaluation might be needed? ☒ Yes ☐ No *Notes:*	Who: Assistive Technology____ Evaluator from Dept. of Ed.___ What: Assistive Technology____ Evaluation_____ By when: February (initial stage)	

Figure 4.14. **Tier III Academic Screening Form.**

Information based on the Academic Screening Form was used to help guide the team's planning of the next steps. Specifically, a comprehensive medical and neurological evaluation was recommended to rule out possible underlying conditions that might be impacting Andrew's performance. A developmental pediatrician and a neurologist evaluated Andrew, and no medical or neurological conditions were identified; however, the neurologist suggested that he be evaluated further for possible dysgraphia or another learning disability that may be impacting his processing skills.

Additionally, the team recommended that an assistive technology evaluation be conducted to determine whether Andrew might benefit from the use of an alternative method of producing written work. Results from this evaluation revealed that it would be beneficial for Andrew to learn how to type, with the long-term goal of having him use an electronic device (i.e., a laptop or iPad) as an alternative to handwriting his assignments. In the short term, he was provided with an AlphaSmart, a simplified version of a laptop computer that functions primarily for word-processing and has been found to be useful for students with graphomotor challenges (www.neo-direct.com). His teachers incorporated this tool into various lessons and activities throughout the day, as they worked individually with him to help him learn how to use it, and encouraged him to utilize the device during writing activities. Andrew's parents also worked with him to improve his typing skills, as he was able to use the home computer to complete his homework assignments that involved written tasks.

A functional behavior assessment (FBA) was conducted to determine the function of Andrew's targeted behavior and help the team develop a more pointed plan to address his areas of difficulty. Observational data were collected by teachers and other team members and recorded on SABC Charts, and the team collaborated with Andrew's parents to complete a Functional Behavior Assessment Interview, which provided valuable information.

Results from the FBA revealed that Andrew's interfering behavior (i.e., verbalizing and off-task/easily distracted behaviors) was functioning largely as (a) escape/avoidance from difficult, disliked tasks and activities, and (b) self-stimulatory/internally motivated purposes. The team generated the following hypothesis to describe the relationships between the factors triggering and maintaining his behavior. See Figure 4.15 Functional Behavior Assessment Interview for Andrew.

> *Andrew engages in verbalizations when he becomes distracted by his inner thoughts, because by doing so he delays/avoids having to complete a difficult/disliked task or a transition that he finds distressing. This is more likely to happen during writing-related tasks that are difficult and disliked and when expectations are unclear or he is in a crowded/loud/overstimulating environment.*

Functional Behavior Assessment Interview Form (Abridged Version)
(Adapted from Dunlap et al., 2010; O'Neill et al., 1997)

Student's Name: _Andrew N._   Date of Interview: _January 2013_

Person(s) Interviewed: _School team and parents_   Interviewer: _Teachers_

Age: _8 years old_   Grade: _3rd_

BACKGROUND INFORMATION

1. What are the student's strengths, skills, and interests (specify highly preferred events, items, people, activities)? _He loves music, particularly The Beatles, and plays the cello at a college level (he has been taking lessons since kindergarten)_

2. What are the student's challenges and areas of greatest difficulty? _Maintaining his focus on difficult/disliked tasks, perspective taking, writing (graphomotor difficulties and challenges with organizing, planning, producing written work)_

3. What people, things, and activities does the student like most? _He has a best friend (in the other 3rd-grade classroom, whom he has been close with since kindergarten); he has a twin brother, and they both enjoy music; he is eager to please adults and positively responds to praise; making connection with him about music (The Beatles) greatly helps establish rapport_

4. What people, things, and activities does the student like the least? _Writing activities; physically demanding tasks (he does not like adapted physical education – he has low arousal level and tends to complain of fatigue frequently)._

BEHAVIOR(S) OF CONCERN

1. Target behaviors interfering with learning and social functioning (in order of priority):

Target Behavior	Description (Operational definition)	Frequency (Circle one)	Duration (Average)	Intensity (Circle one)
Verbalizations	*He talks to himself out loud and without regard for the appropriateness or relevance of his comments; often disrupts others or interrupts (he doesn't realize someone else is speaking, it is not his turn, or that no one is listening/responding to his commentary).*	**Multiple times a day** Once a day Less than once a day	*Continuously*	**High** Medium Low
Off-task, distracted (lack of completing routines, producing work)	*He is unable to start and/or complete common classroom routines (e.g., unpacking) and independent work; easily distracted by inner thoughts – cause him to stop working, and he ends up getting "stuck" thinking about unrelated topics (often his special interest areas); his production of work is significantly below the expected level, and he needs a great deal of teacher attention to keep redirecting him.*	**Multiple times a day** Once a day Less than once a day	*Continuously*	**High** Medium Low

Figure 4.15. **Functional Behavior Assessment Interview Form (Bleiweiss & Tanol, 2012).**

2. If multiple behaviors are listed, do these behaviors occur together in a predictable sequence? If so, briefly describe. *His off-task behaviors (easily distracted by inner thoughts) typically precede his verbalizations, as he begins to verbalize the thoughts that are distracting him; the longer he engages in the running commentary, the louder and more intense his verbalizing becomes.*

3. **Precursor Behavior(s):** Identify any indicators (e.g., low-level disruptive behaviors, or a chain of behaviors) that reliably precede the target behavior. *He often stops whatever he is doing and begins to stare off in the distance and seems to become distracted by something he is thinking about (usually a video game or something related to a special interest area). He starts to verbalize his thoughts, engaging in a running commentary about the topic (that is unrelated to the current task) or repeating a dialogue from something he was watching or from a video game). His verbalizations become louder and he becomes more animated by sometimes adding physical actions related to the game or scene he is replaying. It is difficult for his teachers to redirect him back to task, and his behaviors often disrupt his classmates, as he gets very loud and at times tries to engage them in the "conversation" (he does not actually engage in back-and-forth conversation with them, but speaks to them and does not give them an opportunity to respond).*

PREVENT COMPONENT: Part I – Identifying Setting Events

1a. Are there circumstances **unrelated to the school setting** that occur on some days and not other days that may make interfering behavior more likely?
☐ *Illness (specify)* ☐ *Allergies* ☐ *Missed dose of medication* ☐ *Change in medication*
☒ *Sleep difficulties* ☐ *Fatigue* ☐ *Hunger/thirst* ☐ *Restricted/specialized diet*
☐ *Biomedical supplements* ☐ *Diet change* ☐ *Hormonal changes/menses* ☒ *Change in routine*
☐ *Home conflict* ☐ *Parent not home* ☐ *Bus conflict*
☐ *Sensory sensitivities (specify)*_____
☒ *Other (specify)   Heightened anxiety*_____

1b. Provide a detailed description for any of the items you checked above. *He has difficulty falling asleep and often wakes up several times a night. Changes in familiar routines are challenging for him; he gets confused and has difficulty expressing this or asking for help.*

2. Are there conditions in the **physical environment** that are associated with a high likelihood of interfering behavior? For example, too warm or too cold, too crowded, too much noise, too chaotic, weather condition
☒ *Yes (specify) Crowded, noisy settings when he is unsure of what he should be doing, or expectations are unclear.*
☐ *No*

3a. Are there **times of the school day** when interfering behavior is **most likely** to occur?
☒ *Yes* ☐ *No*
If yes, what are they?
☒ *Morning* ☒ *Before meals* ☒ *During meals* ☒ *After meals* ☒ *Arrival* ☒ *Afternoon*
☒ *Dismissal* ☒ *Other (specify): Interfering behaviors can occur anytime throughout the day.*

3b. Are there **times of the school day** when interfering behavior is **least likely** to occur?
☒ *Yes* ☐ *No*   If yes, what are they?
☐ *Morning* ☐ *Before meals* ☐ *During meals* ☐ *After meals* ☐ *Arrival* ☐ *Afternoon*
☐ *Dismissal* ☒ *Other (specify): When working 1:1 with adult to redirect early signs of distractibility.*

Figure 4.15. **Functional Behavior Assessment Interview Form** *(cont.).*

4a. Are there **specific activities** during which interfering behavior is **very likely** to occur?
⊠ *Yes*　☐ *No*　If yes, specify.
☐ *Reading/ELA*　⊠ *Writing*　☐ *Math*　⊠ *Science*　⊠ *Independent work*
☐ *Small-group work*　⊠ *Whole group work*　☐ *Riding the bus*　☐ *One-on-one*　☐ *Computer*
⊠ *Recess*　☐ *Lunch*　⊠ *Free time*　⊠ *Peer/cooperative*　⊠ *Centers*
⊠ *Discussions/Q&A*　⊠ *Worksheets*　☐ *Specials (specify)* _____
⊠ *Transitions (specify)*　*All are difficult.*　☐ *Other:*_____

4b. Are there **specific activities** during which cooperative and prosocial behavior is **very likely** to occur?
⊠ *Yes*　☐ *No*　If yes, specify.
☐ *Reading/ELA*　☐ *Writing*　⊠ *Math*　☐ *Science*　☐ *Independent work*
☐ *Small-group work*　☐ *Large-group work*　☐ *Riding the bus*　⊠ *One-on-one*　⊠ *Computer*
☐ *Recess*　☐ *Lunch*　☐ *Free time*　☐ *Peer/cooperative*　☐ *Centers*
☐ *Discussions/Q&A*　☐ *Worksheets*　☐ *Specials (specify)* _____
☐ *Transitions (specify)*_____
⊠ *Other:* _When he is actively engaged with his best friend or his twin (usually talking about their_ _mutually preferred special interests or playing video games)._

5a. Are there **specific classmates or adults** whose proximity is associated with a high likelihood of interfering behavior? ☐ *Yes*　⊠ *No*　If yes, specify.
☐ *Peers (specify)*_____　☐ *Teacher(s) (specify)* _____
☐ *OT*_____　☐ *Speech pathologist*_____
☐ *Bus or lunch aide*_____　☐ *Other school staff (specify)*_____
☐ *Parent/guardian*　☐ *Sibling*　☐ *Other family member (specify)*_____
☐ *Other:*_____

5b. Are there **specific classmates or adults** whose proximity is associated with a high likelihood of cooperative and prosocial behavior? ⊠ *Yes*　☐ *No*　If so, who are they?
⊠ *Peers (specify))* _Jack (friend in other 3rd grade class)_　☐ *Teacher(s) (specify)* _____
☐ *OT*_____　☐ *Speech pathologist*_____
☐ *Bus or lunch aide*_____　☐ *Other school staff (specify)*_____
☐ *Parent/guardian*　☐ *Sibling*　☐ *Other family member (specify)*_____
☐ *Other:*_____

PREVENT COMPONENT: Part II – Identifying Antecedents (Triggers)

1. Are there **specific circumstances** that are associated with a high likelihood of interfering behavior (i.e., identify antecedents that are most likely to set off or trigger the behavior). Check all that apply.
☐ *Instructed to start task*　⊠ *Task too difficult*　☐ *Novel task*
☐ *Task is repetitive (same daily)*　☐ *Being told work is wrong*　☐ *Task too long*
☐ *Task is boring*　⊠ *Instructed to transition*　☐ *Reprimand or correction*
☐ *Told "no," "stop," "don't"*　⊠ *Instructed to "wait"*　⊠ *Unstructured time (down time)*
☐ *Seated near specific peer*　☐ *Peer teasing or comments*　⊠ *Change in schedule*
⊠ *Start of nonpreferred activity*　☐ *Denied access to preferred item*　☐ *Removal of preferred item*
☐ *End of preferred activity*　☐ *Unable to complete task*　⊠ *Given unclear directions*
☐ *Communication not understood by others*
☐ *Sudden or unexpected sensory overstimulation (e.g., loud noise, bumped/touched by someone)*
☐ *Teacher is attending to others (reduced level of attention given)*
☐ *Presence or absence of certain person*_____
☐ *Other:* _____

Figure 4.15. Functional Behavior Assessment Interview Form *(cont.).*

TEACH COMPONENT: Part I – Identifying the Function of the Target Behavior

1. Does the interfering behavior seem to be exhibited in order to:
   - **Gain attention from peers or adults**?
     - ☒ Yes *(list the specific peers and/or adults)* *The teacher needs to constantly redirect him back to task; peers tell him to stop interrupting/be quiet.*
     - ☐ No
   - **Obtain access to certain objects or activities** (e.g., toys or games, materials, food)?
     - ☐ Yes *(list specific objects)* _____
     - ☒ No
   - **Delay (escape/avoid) a transition** from a preferred activity to a nonpreferred activity?
     - ☒ Yes *(list specific transition)* *Any transition in which it is unclear what he is expected to do; transitioning to challenging/less preferred task.*
     - ☐ No
   - **Terminate or delay (escape/avoid)** a non-preferred (e.g., difficult, boring, repetitive) task/activity?
     - ☒ Yes *(list specific tasks/activities)* *Writing-related tasks; any long activities where he is not actively engaged or directly involved (e.g., group lessons, down time).*
     - ☐ No
   - **Get away from (escape/avoid)** attention from a nonpreferred classmate or adult?
     - ☐ Yes *(list the specific peers or adults)* _____
     - ☒ No

TEACH COMPONENT: Part II – Identifying Replacement Skills/Behavior

1. What **social skill(s)** could the student learn in order to reduce the likelihood of the interfering behavior occurring in the future?

☐ *Peer interaction*	☐ *Sharing objects*	☒ *Taking turns*
☐ *Play skills*	☐ *Sharing attention*	☐ *Accepting differences*
☐ *Joint or shared attention*	☒ *Conversation skills*	☐ *Making prosocial statements*
☐ *Waiting for reinforcement*	☐ *Getting attention appropriately*	☐ *Losing gracefully*
☐ *Other:* _____		

2. What **interfering-solving skill(s)** could the student learn in order to reduce the likelihood of the interfering behavior occurring in the future?

☒ *Recognizing need for help*	☐ *Note-taking strategies*	☒ *Staying engaged*
☒ *Assignment management*	☒ *Working independently*	☐ *Working with a peer*
☐ *Ignoring peers*	☒ *Graphic organizers*	☐ *Making an outline*
☐ *Self-management*	☐ *Making choices from options*	
☒ *Using visual supports to work independently*		
☒ *Move ahead to easier items, then go back to difficult items*		
☐ *Other:* _____		

3. What **communication skill(s)** could the student learn in order to reduce the likelihood of the interfering behavior occurring in the future?

☒ *Asking for a break*	☐ *Raising hand for attention*	☒ *Asking for help*	☒ *Requesting information*
☐ *Requesting wants*	☐ *Expressing likes & dislikes*	☒ *Active listening*	☒ *Commenting*
☒ *Responding to others*	☐ *Expressing emotions (frustration, anger, hurt)*		
	☐ *Other:* _____		

***Figure 4.15.* Functional Behavior Assessment Interview Form (*cont.*).**

REINFORCE COMPONENT: Part I – Identifying Consequences (Responses)

1. What **consequence(s)** usually follow the student's interfering behavior (i.e., identify particular responses/consequences that are most likely to follow the target behavior)? Check all that apply.
    ⊠ *Given teacher attention*   ⊠ *Redirected*   ⊠ *Reminded of rules/expectations*
    ☐ *Verbal reprimand/warning*   ☐ *Correction*   ⊠ *Assistance given*
    ☐ *Calming/soothing comments provided*   ☐ *Physical prompt*
    ⊠ *Peer attention/reaction (e.g., laughing, negative reaction, reprimand, encouragement) Specify:_____*
    ☐ *Behavior ignored (i.e., attention withdrawn/removed)*
    ☐ *Given personal space (time to chill out/relax)*
    ☐ *Given access to an object/activity*
    ☐ *Request or directive delayed*   ⊠ *Request or directive (demand) withdrawn*
    ⊠ *Delay in activity/task*   ☐ *Activity/task changed*   ⊠ *Activity/task terminated*
    ☐ *Removed from activity or area*   ☐ *Removed object or preferred item*
    ☐ *Removal of reinforcers*   ☐ *Sent to office*   ☐ *Sent home*
    ☐ *Natural consequences (specify) _____*
    ☐ *Other: _____*

2. What is the likelihood of the student's **appropriate behavior** (e.g., on-task behavior, cooperation, successful performance) resulting in acknowledgment or praise from teachers or other school staff?
    ☐ *Very likely*   ⊠ *Sometimes*   ☐ *Seldom*   ☐ *Never*

3. What is the likelihood of the student's **interfering behavior** resulting in acknowledgment (e.g., reprimands, corrections) from teachers or other school staff?
    ⊠ *Very likely*   ☐ *Sometimes*   ☐ *Seldom*   ☐ *Never*

REINFORCE COMPONENT: Part II – Preference Assessment (Identifying Reinforcers)

1. What school-related items and activities are **most enjoyable** to the student? What items or activities could serve as special rewards?
    ☐ *Receives praise from adult*   ☐ *Receives praise from peer*   ⊠ *iPad*   ☐ *Puzzles*
    ☐ *Social interaction with adults*   ☐ *Social interaction with peers*   ⊠ *Music*   ☐ *Art activity*
    ☐ *Helping teacher*   ☐ *Extra free time*   ☐ *Reading*   ☐ *Playing a game*
    ☐ *Going outside*   ⊠ *Video games*   ⊠ *Computer* ⊠ *Watching TV/video*
    ☐ *Going for a walk*   ☐ *Sensory activity (specify) _____*
    ☐ *Food (specify) _____*
    ☐ *Objects (specify) _____*

2. Describe any other items, events, activities, or special interest topics/areas that are particularly motivating for the child. *Spending time with his best friend to talk about their mutual special interest areas; playing video and computer games with his friend or his brother; talking to teacher/speech pathologist about The Beatles; playing on computer or video games; listening to music; playing the cello.*

Figure 4.15. Functional Behavior Assessment Interview Form *(cont.).*

Additional Information

1. What has been tried to address these behaviors?

Brief Description	What Happened?	How Long Was It Tried?
Redirecting him back to task	*He momentarily stops verbalizing but gets distracted again and it starts*	*Since the first day of school (several months)*
Ignoring his verbalizations	*He gets louder and more animated and causes more disruption in the class*	*Several days (sporadically)*
Changing the location of his seat (closer to teacher, away from distractions)	*No change in his behavior*	*His seat was changed several months ago*

Summary of Data From SABC Forms and Functional Behavior Assessment Interview

Attach completed SABC Behavior Forms and provide an analysis of the data collected from those observation records and from the Functional Behavior Assessment Interview.

Student's Name: _Andrew N._ **Date:** _January 2013_

Setting Events: Describe the biological, environmental, and/or social factors that appear to increase the likelihood that the interfering target behavior(s) will occur.

Biological, Social/Emotional Setting Events: *Sleep difficulties (falling asleep, frequently wakes up multiple times a night); tendency to experience heightened anxiety (manifested by repetitive thoughts, preoccupation with what is distressing him).*

Environmental/Activity/Routine Setting Events: *Change in routine; unexpected schedule change; noisy, crowded settings; expectations/directions unclear; disorganized settings cause him to become highly distracted, he reports feeling overwhelmed and starts to focus on his inner thoughts. Writing challenges (possible dysgraphia) increase the aversiveness of tasks requiring him to write, which increases the likelihood that he will shut down and focus on inner thoughts and/or begin to verbalize about unrelated topics.*

Antecedents: Events that occur immediately before the behavior, triggering it: *Asked to start a difficult, disliked routine (e.g., unpack your book bag) in which expectations are unclear (he does not understand what to do, or the steps involved). Instructed to begin writing assignment; bored/prolonged periods of low engagement while working in a group – he begins to verbalize (i.e., making comments that are out of context and inappropriate to the activity).*

Consequences: Events that occur after the behavior occurs, maintaining it: *When he verbalizes, he is reminded to focus on his work or redirected to use quiet voice (keep his thoughts to himself). When he gets distracted and does not complete a routine or task, he is redirected back to task.*

Hypothesized Function(s) of the Target Behaviors

_____Andrew_____ engages in ___verbalizations___ when _he becomes distracted by inner thoughts_
[Student's Name]   [Interfering Behavior]   [Antecedent]

because when he does, _he delays/avoids completing a difficult/disliked task or transition_ . This is more likely
                        [Typical Consequence]

to happen during _writing or other difficult activities_ and/or when _expectations are unclear, or he is in_
                  [Context]   [Setting Events]

crowded/loud/over stimulating settings.
[Setting Events]

Primary Function(s) of the Target Behavior: *Escape/avoidance and internal reinforcement (internally motivated behavior)*

Figure 4.15. **Functional Behavior Assessment Interview Form** ***(cont.).***

At this point, the team completed the Tier III Checklist of Strategies and Supports for Individual Students (Figure 4.16) and identified additional strategies in the behavioral and academic domains, which were still in need of more intense and individualized support.

Tier III
ASD Nest Program
Three-Tier Model

Tier III Strategies and Supports: *Intensive, Individualized Interventions & Consultation*

The strategies outlined below are used to guide the design of an intensive intervention plan for the student. Team members should identify the strategies across all four domains that are most relevant to help support the student. For each of those strategies, indicate whether it should be continued, modified, or added to the student's intervention plan by placing a checkmark in the appropriate column, in accordance with the key below. Comments on implementation recommendations may be added in the column on the right, entitled "Notes on Implementation."

Recommendations		
C	**M**	**A**
Continue *current use of support*	**Modify** *existing support (Increase or decrease)*	**Add** *as a new support*

Student Name: Andrew N.   **Date:** Wednesday, January 8, 2013

Sensory Functioning & Self-Regulation Supports	Identify Strategies That Are Most Relevant			Notes on Implementation
	C	M	A	
1. Provide intensive use of individual, 1:1 sensory-based strategies throughout the day on a consistent schedule with consistent teacher support and data collection with monitoring by OT to evaluate effectiveness.				
2. Provide individual <u>sensory schedule</u> with frequent breaks that require specific sensory input (e.g., proprioception, movement), teacher facilitation, and OT supervision and monitoring.				
3. Implement Break program with scheduled breaks every period.				
4. Provide prompted support/guidance for relaxation training throughout the day.				

Figure 4.16. **Tier III Checklist for Individual Student Planning.**

Behavioral Supports	Identify Strategies That Are Most Relevant			Notes on Implementation
	C	M	A	
1. Use individual task boards/mini-schedules with continued teacher guidance.		✔		Increase use of visual supports (task boards, schedules); teachers need to prompt/ remind him to use them.
2. Provide individualized planned priming for all tasks and events.		✔		Increase frequency of teacher priming him prior to all events, review steps of upcoming transition or activity; make sure he understands what is expected.
3. Provide frequently scheduled teacher-supported break times throughout the day.	✔			Continue providing breaks prior to challenging tasks/ routines.
4. Implement more intensive reinforcement system requiring frequent teacher monitoring.		✔		Increase frequency of reward system; teacher needs to ensure he receives frequent praise and reinforcement.
5. Consider using task simplification as a prevention strategy. (See item #2 under Academic/Curriculum Supports below.)	✔			Continue all Tier I and II task modifications & simplification.

Social Supports	Identify Strategies That Are Most Relevant			Notes on Implementation
	C	M	A	
1. Preview all upcoming social events/activities (e.g., games, special activities, field trips) in 1:1 sessions run by a related service provider.				
2. Provide 1:1 proximity support during challenging social environments with the adult using self-talk/declarative language to facilitate student participation.				
3. Differentiate the use of social support vocabulary and incorporate activities/supports to both develop the concepts underlying the terminology and to improve the students' understanding of social expectations.				

Figure 4.16. Tier III Checklist for Individual Student Planning *(cont.).*

Academic/Curriculum Supports	Identify Strategies That Are Most Relevant			Notes on Implementation
	C	**M**	**A**	
1. **Provide intensive, 1:1 support during lessons or activities/ tasks.**		✔		Increase the frequency of having a teacher (or a related service provider) work with him 1:1 for most academic subjects and during all challenging routines and tasks (e.g., unpacking, packing) to keep him on task and focused.
2. **Modify significantly all content demands, work expectations, and curriculum/instructional pacing.**	✔			Continue modifying all challenging assignments; writing tasks should be differentiated, modified, simplified.
3. **Utilize supplemental programs to address specific academic weaknesses** such as **decoding, computation, or fluency issues.**			✔	Utilize his AlphaSmart to help him type when he experiences difficulty with writing.

Figure 4.16. **Tier III Checklist for Individual Student Planning** *(cont.).*

Essentially, Andrew's team decided to increase the amount of individualized attention and intensity of the strategies that were already in place. They compiled information from the Tier I, Tier II, and Tier III Checklists, the Academic Screening Form, and the Functional Behavior Assessment Interview and created a comprehensive behavior intervention plan that was uniquely tailored to meet Andrew's needs. The completed Summary of Behavior Intervention Strategies is presented in Figure 4.17.

Summary of Behavior Intervention Strategies

Student: _____Andrew N._____ Date: _____January 2013_____

Target Behavior(s):_____Off-task/easily distracted/staring; verbalizations (talking to himself aloud)_____

Prevention Strategies: These strategies involve intervening *prior* to the occurrence of impeding/interfering behavior.

- **Setting Events & Antecedent-Based Strategies** – Each modification is linked to the *Setting Events* and *Antecedents* identified.

Setting Events & Antecedents	Prevention Strategies
Crowded, noisy, chaotic settings; heightened anxiety	Provide headphones, earplugs to reduce noise level
	Use a study carrel ("office")
Expectations, directions are unclear (i.e., he does not know what to do); difficulties with transitions	Priming prior to transitions and challenging routines (preview what to expect, what to do)
	Use visual supports outlining upcoming activities, break down complex tasks/routines into simpler steps, use visual cues of expectations to remind him what to do and to redirect him back to task
	Use concrete, clear language – give him processing time
Easily distracted/difficulty sustaining attention	Use an individual timer to provide him with a concrete representation of time remaining on a task; teachers should prompt him to reference the timer frequently.
	Reduce difficulty/aversiveness of challenging tasks
	Modify expectations with writing tasks (shorten duration, amount of work he is expected to produce)
Instructed to begin challenging or boring tasks (writing)	Intersperse independent writing and teacher note-taking
	Use graphic organizers to help with planning and structuring writing assignments
	Break down routines and tasks into simpler steps – use task sequencing boards
	Take a break prior to starting difficult tasks

Replacement Strategies: These strategies involve *teaching* the student more effective and appropriate means of communicating, coping, and enhancing self-management skills.

Alternative Adaptive Behavior	Replacement Strategies
Teach him typing skills	Allow him to use the AlphaSmart for writing tasks and homework
	Provide individualized instruction to enhance his typing skills (fluency)
Teach him self-regulation skill – to reduce his verbalizations (increase time on task)	Use visual reminders (cuing him to "keep his thoughts to himself")
	Create a series of social narratives aimed at increasing his understanding of the impact of his behavior (verbalizing) on others.
Teach him to request assistance	Functional communication training: HELP cards; use visual cues, teacher prompts to remind him to ask for help when he is not sure what to do or appears to have difficulty with an activity/task
Teach him to request a break	Functional communication training: The Break program, use visuals cues, teacher reminders encouraging him to request a break when he becomes distracted, frustrated, or begins to verbalize

Figure 4.17. **Summary of Behavior Intervention Strategies Form.**

Response Strategies: These strategies modify the ways in which team members respond to both *interfering target behaviors* (decreasing the likelihood that they will occur) and *replacement behaviors* (increasing the likelihood that they will be used consistently).

Response Strategies	
To increase the amount of time he is on task/focused/engaged during classroom activities and routines.	Implement a reward system – he earns stickers (checkmarks) when he is able to remain on task/focused/working on activity or task for increasing intervals of time (e.g., start with 5 mins and increase to 10 mins then 15 mins as he masters each interval)
	Provide behavior-specific praise (catch him being good), highlighting instances when he is on task and when he uses (attempts to use) his coping strategies
To reduce out-of-context/off-task verbalizations	Use visual cues of behavioral expectations to remind him to "keep his thoughts to himself" or to "raise his hand" if he has something to say"
	Provide behavior specific praise (catch him being good), highlighting instances when he is engaged in an activity without verbalizing or when he stops verbalizing upon being redirected

Figure 4.17. **Summary of Behavior Intervention Strategies Form *(cont.).***

The team agreed to keep these strategies and increased level of support in place for several weeks, monitor Andrew's response to these intense supports, and note any signs of progress. They followed up in five weeks to evaluate Andrew's progress and completed the Tier III Implementation Check-In Form (Figure 4.18).

Tier III Implementation Check-In

The first Tier III implementation check-in should take place approximately 3-4 weeks after the student's plan has been implemented. After that, if the student continues to make progress, check-in meetings can take place every 5-6 weeks.

Student: _____ Andrew N _____ **Date:** _____ Wednesday, February 8, 2013 _____

Have the recommended strategies and supports been implemented? Describe when and how.

All of the supports and strategies outlined in Andrew's Summary of Behavioral Intervention Strategies were implemented as described in the plan.

How did the student respond to the interventions? Have any improvements in the previously identified area(s) of concern taken place? If so, describe those changes by giving specific examples.

Andrew responded positively to the elevated level of support provided to him. Having a teacher work 1:1 with him during more challenging tasks such as writing and during difficult routines (e.g., transitions, unpacking, packing up at the end of the day) was extremely helpful in keeping him on task and completing his work in a timely manner. When he did not have that level of support, however, these positive results were not seen. The assistive technology (AlphaSmart device) has been tremendously beneficial for Andrew, and he is becoming more adept at typing. He is beginning to complete his writing assignments using his AlphaSmart, which has significantly helped increase the amount of work he produces. While he still needs a teacher to work with him while he uses his device, it appears to be a very effective support.

Next step(s) in supporting this student: Provide the team's recommendation(s) and identify the person(s) responsible for implementing them.

Continue providing this elevated level of support for Andrew. The teachers will continue to make sure that he has 1:1 support during all challenging tasks and will utilize visual supports and reinforcement procedures, as well as his AlphaSmart device. The team will check back in several weeks to reassess Andrew's progress and discuss next steps based on how he is responding to the strategies and supports.

Figure 4.18. Tier III Implementation Check-In Form.

Although the team recognized that Andrew's verbalizing behavior had been reduced, he still required a great deal of adult individualized attention to remind him to "keep his thoughts to himself" or to "raise his hand if he had something to say." Additionally, his teachers reported that he was able to produce increasingly greater amounts of work, as he was provided with one-to-one attention during more difficult tasks, and the teachers implemented a variety of visual supports and strategies. They also noted that once he became acclimated to the AlphaSmart, he was able to complete more assignments involving writing tasks. However, a teacher still needed to work very closely with him to ensure that he remained on task. Therefore, the team decided to keep Andrew in Tier III in the behavior and academic domains, maintaining the same level of supports and strategies. It was further agreed that they would continue monitoring his progress and reevaluate his responsiveness to the intervention strategies approximately six weeks later.

As the school year drew to a close, Andrew demonstrated substantial progress, albeit with significantly intense levels of support still required. The team decided to keep all supports and strategies in place through the end of the school year and revisit his case when school resumed the following fall. The team also prepared a transition binder, which contained all of the Tier Checklists completed on Andrew, as well as all other relevant paperwork pertaining to his intervention, and shared this material with the teachers and service providers who would be working with him in fourth grade.

References

Aarts, H. (2012). Goals, motivation, social cognition, and behavior. In S. T. Fiske & C. N. (Eds.). *The Sage handbook of social cognition* (pp. 75-96). Thousand Oaks, CA: Sage Publications.

Aspy, R., & Grossman, B. G. (2011). *Designing comprehensive interventions for high-functioning individuals with autism spectrum disorders: The Ziggurat model – Release 2.0.* Shawnee Mission, KS: AAPC Publishing.

Bambara, L. M., & Kern, L. (2005). *Individualized supports for students with problem behaviors: Designing positive behavior plans.* New York, NY: Guilford Press.

Bambara, L. M., Koger, F., Katzer, T., & Davenport, T. A. (1995). Embedding choice in the context of daily routines: An experimental case study. *Journal of the Association for Persons with Severe Handicaps, 20,* 185-195.

Banda, D., & Kubina Jr., R. (2006). The effects of a high-probability request sequencing technique in enhancing transition behaviors. *Education & Treatment of Children, 29*(3), 507-516.

Bellini, S., & Akullian, J. (2007). A meta-analysis of video modeling and video self-modeling interventions for children and adolescents with autism spectrum disorders. *Exceptional Children, 73*(3), 264-287.

Bernard-Opitz, V., & Häußler, A. (2011). *Visual supports for children with autism spectrum disorder: Materials for visual learners.* Shawnee Mission, KS: AAPC Publishing.

Bleiweiss, J. D., & Tanol, G. (2012). *Functional behavior assessment interview (abridged version).* Unpublished manuscript.

Buckley, S., & Newchok, D. (2005). Differential impact of response effort within a response chain on use of mands in a student with autism. *Research in Developmental Disabilities, 26*(1), 77-85.

Buggey, T. (2009). *Seeing is believing: Video self-modeling for people with autism and other developmental disabilities.* Bethesda, MD: Woodbine House.

Buron, K. D., & Curtis, M. (2012). *The incredible 5-point scale* (2nd ed.). Shawnee Mission, KS: AAPC Publishing.

Carr, E. G., & Durand, V. M. (1985). Reducing behavior problems through functional communication training. *Journal of Applied Behavior Analysis, 18,* 111-126.

Carr, E. G., Dunlap, G., Horner, R. H., Koegel, R. L., Turnbull, A. P., Sailor, W., Anderson, C. M., et al. (2002). Positive behavior support: Evolution of an applied science. *Journal of Positive Behavior Interventions, 4,* 4-16.

Cautela, J. R., & Groden, J. (1978). *Relaxation: A comprehensive manual for adults, children, and children with special needs.* Champaign, IL: Research Press.

Centers for Medicare and Medicaid Services. (2010). *Autism spectrum disorders: Final report on environmental scan.* Washington, DC: Author.

Cohen, S., & Hough, L. (Eds.). (2013). *The ASD Nest model: A framework for inclusive education for higher-functioning children with autism spectrum disorders.* Shawnee Mission, KS: AAPC Publishing.

Crimmins, D., Farrell, A. F., Smith, P. W., & Bailey, A. (2007). *Positive strategies for students with behavior problems.* Baltimore, MD: Paul H. Brookes Publishing Co.

Dadds, M., Schwartz, S., Adams, R., & Rose, S. (1988). The effects of social context and verbal skill on the stereotypic and task-involved behavior of autistic children. *Journal of Child Psychology & Psychiatry, 29*(5), 669-676.

Delano, M., & Snell, M. E. (2006).The effects of Social Stories™ on the social engagement of children with autism. *Journal of Positive Behavior Interventions, 8*, 29-42.

Dettmer, S., Simpson, R. L., Myles, B. S., & Ganz, J. L. (2000). The use of visual supports to facilitate transitions of students with autism. *Focus on Autism and Other Developmental Disabilities, 15*, 163-169.

Dunlap, G., Iovannone, R., Kincaid, D., Wilson, K., Christiansen, K., Strain, P., & English, C. (2010). *Prevent teach reinforce: The school-based model of individualized positive behavior support.* Baltimore, MD: Brookes Publishing.

Durand, V. M., & Merges, E. (2001). Functional communication training: A contemporary behavior analytic intervention for problem behaviors. *Focus on Autism and Other Developmental Disabilities, 16*, 110-119.

Friend, M., & Cook, L. (2012). *Interactions: Collaboration skills for school professionals, 6th ed.* Boston, MA: Allyn & Bacon.

Fuchs, D., & Fuchs, L. S. (2006). Introduction to response to intervention: What, why, and how valid is it? *Reading Research Quarterly, 41*, 93-99.

Fuchs, D., Fuchs, L. S., & Compton D. L. (2012). Smart RTI: A next-generation approach to multilevel prevention. *Exceptional Children, 78*(3), 263-279.

Gagnon, E. (2001). *Power cards: Using special interests to motivate children and youth with Asperger syndrome and autism.* Shawnee Mission, KS: AAPC Publishing.

Glaeser, B. C., Pierson, M. R., & Fritschman, N. (2003). Comic Strip Conversations™: A positive behavioral support strategy. *Teaching Exceptional Children, 36*(2), 14-19.

Gray, C. (1994). *Comic Strip Conversations™: Colorful, illustrated interactions with students with autism and related disorders.* Arlington, TX: Future Horizons.

Gray, C. (2010). *The new Social Story™ book: Revised and expanded 10th anniversary edition.* Arlington, TX: Future Horizons.

Gutstein, S. E., & Sheeley, R. K. (2002). *Relationship development intervention with young children: Social and emotional developmental activities for Asperger syndrome, autism, PDD and NLD.* Philadelphia, PA: Jessica Kingsley Publishers.

Harper, C., Symon, J., & Frea, W. (2008). Recess is time-in: Using peers to improve social skills of children with autism. *Journal of Autism & Developmental Disorders, 38*(5), 815-826.

Henry, S., & Smith Myles, B. (2013). *The comprehensive autism planning system [CAPS] for individuals with autism spectrum disorders and related disabilities; Integrating evidence-based practices throughout the student's day* (2nd ed.). Shawnee Mission, KS: AAPC Publishing.

Hodgdon, L. A. (1995). *Visual strategies for improving communication: Practical supports for school and home.* Troy, MI: Quirk Roberts Publishing.

Hodgdon, L. A. (1999). *Solving behavior problems in autism: Improving communication with visual strategies.* Troy, MI: Quirk Roberts Publishing.

Horner, R. H., Dunlap, G., Koegel, R. L., Carr, E. G., Sailor, W., Anderson, J., Albin, R. W., & O'Neill, R. E. (1990). Toward a technology of "nonaversive" behavioral support. *Journal of the Association for Persons with Severe Handicaps, 15*, 125-132.

Kabot, S., & Reeve, C. (2010). *Setting up classroom spaces that support students with autism spectrum disorders.* Shawnee Mission, KS: AAPC Publishing.

Kamps, D., Wills, H. P., Heitzman-Powell, L., Laylin, J., Szoke, C., Petrillo, T., & Culey, A. (2011). Class-wide function-related intervention teams: Effects of group contingency programs in urban classrooms. *Journal of Positive Behavior Interventions, 13*(3), 154-167.

Keeling, K., Myles, B., Gagnon, E., & Simpson, R. (2003). Using the Power Card strategy to teach sportsmanship skills to a child with autism. *Focus on Autism & Other Developmental Disabilities, 18*(2), 103.

Kern, L., Marder, T. J., Boyajian, A. E., Elliot, C. M., & McElhattan, D. (1997). Augmenting the independence of self-management procedures by teaching self-initiation across settings and activities. *School Psychology Quarterly, 12*, 23-32.

Kern, P., Wolery, M., & Aldridge, D. (2007). Use of songs to promote independence in morning greeting routines for young children with autism. *Journal of Autism & Developmental Disorders, 37*(7), 1264-1271.

Kluth, P. (2010). *"You're going to love this kid!:" Teaching students with autism in the inclusive classroom.* Baltimore, MD: Paul H. Brookes Publishing Company.

Koegel, L., Koegel, R., Frea, W., & Green-Hopkins, I. (2003). Priming as a method of coordinating educational services for students with autism. *Language, Speech, & Hearing Services in Schools, 34*, 228-235.

Koegel, L. K., Koegel, R. L., Hurley, C., & Frea, W. D. (1992). Improving social skills and disruptive behavior in children with autism through self-management. *Journal of Applied Behavior Analysis, 25*, 341-353.

Koegel, R. L.,Camarate, S., Koegel, L. K., Bea-Tall, A., & Smith, A. E. (1988). Increasing speech intelligibility in children with autism. *Journal of Autism and Developmental Disorders, 28*(3), 241-251.

Koegel, R. L., Dyer, K., & Bell, L. K. (1987). The influence of child-preferred activities on autistic children's speech behavior. *Journal of Applied Behavior Analysis, 20*, 243-252.

Koegel, R. L., & Koegel, L. K. (1990). Extended reductions in stereotypic behavior of students with autism through a self-management treatment package. *Journal of Applied Behavior Analysis, 23*, 119-127.

Kokina, A., & Kern, L. (2010). Social Story™ interventions for students with autism spectrum disorders: A meta-analysis. *Journal of Autism and Developmental Disorders, 40*, 812-826.

LaBelle, C., & Charlop-Christy, M. (2002). Individualizing functional analysis to assess multiple and changing functions of severe behavior problems in children with autism. *Journal of Positive Behavior Interventions, 4*(4), 231-241.

Lequia, J., Machalicek, W., & Rispoli, M. J. (2012). Effects of activity schedules on challenging behavior exhibited in children with autism spectrum disorders: A systematic review. *Research in Autism Spectrum Disorders, 6*, 480-492.

Lucyshyn, J. M., Albin, R. W., Horner, R. H., Mann, J. C., Mann, J. A., & Wadsworth, G. (2007). Family implementation of positive behavior support for a child with autism: Longitudinal, single-case, experimental, and descriptive replication and extension. *Journal of Positive Behavior Interventions, 9*(3), 131-150.

Mancil, G. R. (2006). Functional communication training: A review of the literature related to children with autism. *Education and Training in Developmental Disabilities, 41*(3), 213-224.

Marcus, B. A., & Vollmer, T. R. (1996). Combining contingent reinforcement and differential reinforcement schedules as treatment for aberrant behavior. *Journal of Applied Behavior Analysis, 29*, 43-51.

Matson, J. L., & Taras, M. E. (1989). A 20-year review of punishment and alternative methods to treat problem behaviors in developmentally delayed persons. *Research in Developmental Disabilities, 10*, 85-104.

Mesibov, G. B., Browder, D. M., & Kirkland, C. (2002). Using individualized schedules as a component of positive behavioral support for students with developmental disabilities. *Journal of Positive Behavior Interventions, 4*, 73-79.

Mullins, J. L., & Christian, L. (2001). The effects of progressive relaxation training on the disruptive behavior of a boy with autism. *Research in Developmental Disabilities, 22,* 449-462.

Myles, B. S. (2005). *Children and youth with Asperger Syndrome: Strategies for success in inclusive settings.* Thousand Oaks, CA: Corwin Press.

Myles, B. S., & Southwick, J. (2005). *Asperger syndrome and difficult moments: Practical solutions for tantrums, rage, and meltdowns* (2nd ed.). Shawnee Mission, KS: AAPC Publishing.

Myles, B. S., Trautman, M. L., & Schelvan, R. L. (2013). *The hidden curriculum for understanding unstated rules in social situations for adolescents and young adults* (2nd ed.). Shawnee Mission, KS: AAPC Publishing.

National Autism Center (NAC). (2009). *National standards report: Addressing the need for evidence-based practice guidelines for autism spectrum disorders.* Randolph, MA: Author.

National Professional Development Center on Autism Spectrum Disorders (NPDC on ASD). (n.d.). *Evidence-based practice briefs.* Retrieved from http://autismpdc.fpg.unc.edu/content/briefs

O'Neill, R. E. (2005). Toward a technology of "nonaversive" behavioral support. *Research and Practice for Persons with Severe Disabilities, 30*(1), 3-10. (Reprinted from *The Journal of the Association for the Severely Handicapped, 15*(3), 1990.)

O'Neill, R. E., Horner, R. H., Albin, R. W., Sprague, J. R., Storey, K., & Newton, J. S. (1997). *Functional assessment and program development for problem behavior: A practical handbook* (2nd ed.). Pacific Grove, CA: Brooks/Cole.

Owen-DeSchryver, J., Carr, E. G., Cale, S., & Blakeley-Smith, A. (2008). Promoting social interactions between students with autism spectrum disorders and their peers in inclusive school settings. *Focus on Autism & Other Developmental Disabilities, 23*(1), 15-28.

Piazza, C., Moes, D., & Fisher, W. (1996). Differential reinforcement of alternative behavior and demand fading in the treatment of escape-maintained destructive behavior. *Journal of Applied Behavior Analysis, 29*(4), 569-572.

Pierce, K., & Schreibman, L. (1997). Multiple peer use of pivotal response training to increase social behaviors of classmates with autism: Results from trained and untrained peers. *Journal of Applied Behavior Analysis, 30,* 157-160.

Pierce, K. L., & Schreibman, L. (1994). Teaching daily living skills to children with autism in unsupervised settings through pictorial self-management. *Journal of Applied Behavior Analysis, 27,* 471-481.

Quill, K. A. (1997). Instructional considerations for young children with autism: The rationale for visually cued instruction. *Journal of Autism and Developmental Disorders, 27,* 697-714.

Reaven, J., Blakeley-Smith, A., Leuthe, E., Moody, E., & Hepburn, S. (2012). Facing your fears in adolescence: Cognitive-behavioral therapy for high-functioning autism spectrum disorders and anxiety. *Autism Research and Treatment, 2012,* 1-13.

Reichle, J., Drager, K., & Davis, C. (2002). Using requests to obtain desired items and to gain release from nonpreferred activities: Implications for assessment and intervention. *Education and Treatment of Children, 25*(1), 47-66.

Scattone, D., Tingstrom, D. H., & Wilczynski, S. M. (2006). Increasing appropriate social interactions of children with autism spectrum disorders using Social Stories™. *Focus on Autism and Other Developmental Disabilities, 21,* 211-222.

Scheuermann, B. K. (2012). *Positive behavior supports for the classroom.* Upper Saddle River, NJ: Pearson Education.

Schilling, D. L., & Schwartz, I. S. (2004). Alternative seating for young children with autism spectrum disorder: Effects on classroom behavior. *Journal of Autism and Developmental Disorders, 34*(4), 423-432.

Shogren, K. A., Faggella-Luby, M. N., Bae, S., & Wehmeyer, M. L. (2004). The effect of choice-making as an intervention for problem behavior: A meta-analysis. *Journal of Positive Behavior Interventions, 5,* 228-237.

Shukla-Mehta, S., Miller, T., & Callahan, K. (2010). Evaluating the effectiveness of video instruction on social and communication skills training for children with autism spectrum disorders: A review of the literature. *Focus on Autism & Other Developmental Disabilities, 25*(1), 23-36.

Smith, S., Myles, B. S., Aspy, R., Grossman, B. G., & Henry, S. A. (2010). Sustainable change in quality of life for individuals with ASD: Using a comprehensive planning process. *Focus on Exceptional Children, 43*(3), 1-22.

Stahmer, A. C., & Schreibman, L. (1992). Teaching children with autism appropriate play in unsupervised environments using a self-management treatment package. *Journal of Applied Behavior Analysis, 25,* 447-459.

Stansberry-Brusnahan, L. L., & Collet-Klingenberg, L. L. (2010). Evidence-based practices for young children with autism spectrum disorders: Guidelines and recommendations from the National Resource Council and National Professional Development Center on Autism Spectrum Disorders. *International Journal of Early Childhood Special Education, 2,* 45-56.

Steen, P. L., & Zuriff, G. E. (1977). The use of relaxation in the treatment of self-injurious behavior. *Journal of Behavior Therapy and Experimental Psychiatry, 18,* 447-448.

Sterling-Turner, H., & Jordan, S. (2007). Interventions addressing transition difficulties for individuals with autism. *Psychology in the Schools, 44*(7), 681-690.

Stück, M., & Gloeckner, N. (2005, May). Yoga for children in the mirror of the science: Working spectrum and practice fields of the training of relaxation with elements of yoga for children. *Early Child Development and Care, 175*(4), 371-377.

Van DerHeyden, A. M., & Burns, M. K. (2010). *Essentials of response to intervention.* Hoboken, NJ: Wiley.

Wilde, L. D., Koegel, L. K., & Koegel, R. L. (1992). *Increasing success in school through priming: A training manual.* Santa Barbara, CA: University of California.

Winner, M. G. (2005). *Think social: A social thinking curriculum for school-age students.* San Jose, CA: Michelle Garcia Winner Publishing.

Winner, M. G. (2007). *Thinking about you thinking about me: Philosophy and strategies to further develop perspective taking and communicative abilities for persons with social cognitive deficits.* San Jose, CA: Michelle Garcia Winner Publishing.

Zhang, J., & Wheeler, J. (2011). A meta-analysis of peer-mediated interventions for young children with autism spectrum disorders. *Education and Training in Autism and Developmental Disabilities, 46*(1), 62-77.

About the Authors

Jamie Bleiweiss, PhD, is an assistant professor in the Department of Special Education at Hunter College, where she teaches in the Early Childhood Special Education master's degree program. She is also the director of the Summer Training Institute for new staff of the ASD Nest program. Specializing in work with children diagnosed with autism spectrum disorders, Dr. Bleiweiss has extensive clinical experience with children, families, and professionals in a variety of community and educational settings, and has served as a behavior consultant for several agencies and programs in the New York metropolitan area. Professor Bleiweiss teaches two graduate courses on autism spectrum disorders at Hunter College and has presented numerous workshops and inservice training sessions on topics related to ASD, challenging behavior, and positive behavior support. Dr. Bleiweiss serves as a behavior specialist for the NYC Department of Education's ASD Nest program and consults with a variety of community-based organizations, theatres, and local businesses, providing training and support in an effort to create greater opportunities for individuals with autism and their families to be more meaningfully included within their communities and take part in valued leisure and recreational activities. She is also the author of the chapter "Positive Behavior Support" and is a co-author of the chapter "The ASD Nest Classroom" along with Shirley Cohen and Lauren Hough in *The ASD Nest Model* (2013) published by AAPC Publishing.

Lauren Hough, MSEd, is director of professional development for the ASD Nest Support Project at New York University's Steinhardt School of Culture, Education, and Human Development. She provides professional development workshops, school-based consultation, and seminars on meeting the needs of school-aged students on the spectrum in inclusion settings. She has also worked with Shirley Cohen to create intervention guidelines for the ASD Nest program, and is co-editor and contributing author of the book *The ASD Nest Model* (2013) published by AAPC Publishing. Ms. Hough's primary area of focus is the cognitive profiles of students on the autism spectrum, specifically how academic strengths and challenges can be rooted in issues related to weaknesses in theory of mind and executive functioning. She is also interested in how recognizing and building on students' strengths, interests, and talents can maximize their academic experiences, and she and two colleagues have recently authored an article in the journal *Intervention in School and Clinic* (2012, volume 3, issue 47) on this topic, "Case Studies on Using Strengths and Interests to Address the Needs of Students with Autism Spectrum Disorders." Ms. Hough also works privately as a learning specialist and social group facilitator, and she consults with schools outside the ASD Nest program network as well as other organizations supporting individuals on the autism spectrum.

Shirley Cohen, PhD, a professor in the Department of Special Education at Hunter College for many years, became professor emeritus in 2011. In her role at Hunter College Dr. Cohen directed the ASD Nest training program under contract from the NYC Department of Education for six years. She also served as the first director of the Regional Center for Autism Spectrum Disorders at Hunter and held numerous administrative roles at the college such as chairperson of the Department of Special Education, assistant dean, associate dean, and interim dean of the School of Education. Dr. Cohen co-developed the ASD Nest program for the NYC public schools with Dorothy Siegel and continues to serve as a consultant and intervention developer for the program. She is the author of the book *Targeting Autism,* originally published in 1998 and since 2006 in its third edition, as well as two earlier books on disability. In addition, she is an editor and contributing author of the book *The ASD Nest Model* published by AAPC in 2013. Professor Cohen has directed federal, state, city, and private foundation grants in the area of disability and has served as a mentor to numerous teachers and other young leaders in the field of autism intervention in NYC.

PUBLISHING

P.O. Box 23173
Shawnee Mission, Kansas 66283-0173
www.aapcpublishing.net

CPSIA information can be obtained
at www.ICGtesting.com
Printed in the USA
BVHW051354010921
615691BV00013B/335

9 781937 473815